A Study on the Acquisition of English Function-chains:
A Focus on Japanese EFL Learners

A Study on the Acquisition of English Function-chains: A Focus on Japanese EFL Learners

Yoko Fujiwara

KEISUISHA
Hiroshima, Japan
2007

Copyright © 2007 Yoko Fujiwara

Published in Japan by Keisuisha,Co.,Ltd.
1-4 Komachi, Naka-ku, Hiroshima 730-0041
ISBN978- 4-87440-946-6 C3082

Printed in Japan
2007

TABLE OF CONTENTS

List of Figures and Tables	iv
Acknowledgements	vii
Preface	ix
Chapter 1 Introduction	1
1.1 Background and purpose of the present study	1
1.2 Thesis outline	3
Notes	5
Chapter 2 Literature review	7
2.1 Historical perspective	7
2.1.1 Interlanguage pragmatics in SLA	7
2.1.2 Level of proficiency and pragmatic competence	9
2.1.3 Types of function-chains and pragmatic competence	12
2.2 Sociolinguistic perspective	13
2.3 Conclusions from the literature review and overall research design	17
Notes	19
Chapter 3 Study 1: Junior high students' recognition of the appropriateness of function-chain structures	22
3.1 Objectives	22
3.2 Method	22
3.2.1 Participants	22
3.2.2 Materials	22
3.2.3 Procedure	23
3.3 Results	25
3.3.1 Results of factor analysis	25

3.3.2 Results of Hayashi's quantification model III	28
3.4 Discussion	34
Notes	35

Chapter 4 Study 2: The recognition of the appropriateness of actual utterances by junior high students at two proficiency levels 37

4.1 Objectives	37
4.2 Method	38
4.2.1 Participants and determination of their level of proficiency in English	38
4.2.2 Materials	38
4.2.3 Procedure	39
4.2.4 Scoring	41
4.2.5 Means of analysis	41
4.3 Results	41
4.4 Discussion	44
Notes	45

Chapter 5 Study 3 (Analysis 1): The recognition of the appropriateness of actual utterances by junior high students, university students, and native speakers of English 46

5.1 Objectives	46
5.2 Method	47
5.2.1 Participants	47
5.2.2 Materials	47
5.2.3 Procedure	48
5.2.4 Scoring	49
5.2.5 Means of analysis	49
5.3 Results	50

	5.4 Discussion	60
	Notes	62
Chapter 6	Study 3 (Analysis 2): The acquisition of English function-chains viewed qualitatively	64
	6.1 Objectives	64
	6.2 Method	64
	6.2.1 Participants, materials, procedure, and scoring	64
	6.2.2 Means of analysis	65
	6.3 Results	65
	6.4 Discussion	77
	Notes	81
Chapter 7	Conclusions and remaining problems	83
	7.1 Conclusions and pedagogical implications	83
	7.2 The remaining problems and implications for future research	86

References	89
Appendices	94
Name index	133
Subject index	135

List of Figures and Tables

	Section	Page
Figure 1. Factors influencing appropriateness	(2.2)	16
Figure 2. An example of a function-chain pattern: function 13 to function 14	(3.2.2)	23
Figure 3. The location of each function-chain on the coordinate (X-axis: Dimension I, Y-axis: Dimension II) by using Hayashi's quantification model III	(3.3.2)	29
Figure 4. The location of each function-chain on the coordinate (X-axis: Dimension I, Y-axis: Dimension II) by using Hayashi's quantification model III	(3.3.2)	31
Table 1. An example from the test items	(3.2.3)	24
Table 2. Function-chains with large factor loadings in Factor 1	(3.3.1)	26
Table 3. Function-chains with large factor loadings in Factor 2	(3.3.1)	27
Table 4. Function-chains with large factor loadings in Factor 3	(3.3.1)	27
Table 5. The mean and the standard deviation of the category scores of each group under Dimension I and Dimension II	(3.3.2)	30
Table 6. Category score of each test item (function-chain) by using Hayashi's quantification model III	(3.3.2)	32
Table 7. Function-chains with high category scores in Dimension I	(3.3.2)	33
Table 8. Function-chains with high category scores in Dimension II	(3.3.2)	34
Table 9. Function-chains in this appropriateness judgment test	(4.2.2)	39
Table 10. An example of the Assertion Function-chain test items	(4.2.3)	40
Table 11. Descriptive statistics	(4.3)	42
Table 12. Multivariate tests	(4.3)	42
Table 13. Tests of between-subjects effects	(4.3)	43
Table 14. An example of the Assistance Function-chain test items	(5.2.3)	48

Table 15. Descriptive statistics	(5.3)	50
Table 16. Table of ANOVA	(5.3)	51
Table 17. Simple main effect of interaction between proficiency level and function-chain	(5.3)	52
Table 18. Multiple comparisons of the levels of proficiency for the Assistance Function-chain	(5.3)	53
Table 19. Multiple comparisons of the levels of proficiency for the Expressing Liking Function-chain	(5.3)	54
Table 20. Multiple comparisons of the levels of proficiency for the Assertion Function-chain	(5.3)	55
Table 21. Multiple comparisons of the levels of proficiency for the Reassurance Function-chain	(5.3)	56
Table 22. Multiple comparisons of the levels of proficiency for the Expressing Interest Function-chain	(5.3)	57
Table 23. Multiple comparisons of the function-chains for the U^+ group	(5.3)	59
Table 24. Multiple comparisons of the function-chains for the NS group	(5.3)	59
Table 25. Descriptive statistics	(6.3)	66-68
Table 26. Table of ANOVA	(6.3)	68-70
Table 27. Multiple comparisons of the levels of proficiency for each test item	(6.3)	71
Table 28-1. Function-chains for which scores are lower than those of native speakers (revealing areas of difficulty specific to each group)	(6.3)	73
Table 28-2. Specific function-chains from Table 28-1 that proved difficult for Japanese EFL learners	(6.3)	74-75
Table 29-1. Function-chains for which scores are higher than those of native speakers	(6.3)	76
Table 29-2. Specific function-chains from Table 29-1	(6.3)	76

Acknowledgements

Firstly, I wish to express my sincere gratitude to my academic supervisor and head of the dissertation committee, Dr. Seiji Fukazawa (Hiroshima University), whose encouragement, guidance, and invaluable advice throughout the whole process of writing this dissertation have been very helpful and essential for me.

Professor Yoshiyuki Nakao (Hiroshima University) is another committee member that provided me with many insightful suggestions as well as great encouragement. I highly valued his careful and constructive advice.

I also wish to thank the other dissertation committee members, Professor Shogo Miura, Dr. Toshiaki Mori, and Dr. Kumiko Sakoda, all of Hiroshima University, for their detailed comments, suggestions, and constant support. Without their help, the entire research process would have been much more difficult.

Additionally, I feel deep gratitude to Dr. Toshiaki Ozasa (Fukuyama Heisei University, formerly with Hiroshima University), who helped me find a direction for my research, and provided many thoughtful and helpful comments.

Special thanks goes to Professor Michikazu Kaneda (currently Yasuda Women's University), who has been source of encouragement since I first entered university, and has always urged me to continue on with my studies and research work. Professor Nobuyori Kumagai (Yamaguchi University) has also always been willing to help me at any time when I needed his advice, whether concerning statistics, or any other questions or concerns I had. His suggestions always proved to be on the mark, and were offered with great kindness.

Thanks are also due to Dr. Marilyn Higgins, Associate Professor Robert Schalkoff, Associate Professor Amy Wilson, Adjunct Professor Alan Christ, and Adjunct Professor Steve Gardener (Yamaguchi Prefectural University), Mr. Joseph Snell and Mr. Chris Kilby (ALTs working in the Yamaguchi City public school system), Mr. Kevin Zirkle, Ms. Becky Zirkle, Ms. Mary Zirkle, and Ms. Priscilla Probst (World Gospel Mission), and Ms. Kathy Karam (Maple English School) for their assistance in making test items to assess pragmatic competence. Professor David Le Sage (Yamaguchi University) provided me with the materials on natural discourse. Dr. Nozomu Sonda, Ms. Eva Sonda, and Mr. Duane Levi (One World International) recorded the instructions and dialogues of the test items into CDs.

I wish to express my gratitude to Associate Professor Satoshi Hiramoto and Dr. Hironobu Matsuoka (both of Yasuda Women's University), who helped me establish the contact with the California State University, San Bernardino, through which it became possible to interview their students for the purpose of data collection. I'm grateful to the above university for the permission it granted for data collection, and thanks are due also to Shinonome Junior High School and Mihara Junior High School (both attached to Hiroshima University), which also allowed me to interview their students.

I am indebted to Dr. Hidemasa Nosaki (currently Miyazaki Women's Junior College) for valuable help in analyzing the data collected.

James Humphreys (ALT working in the Yamaguchi City public school system) proofread this paper and gave valuable suggestions.

All of those mentioned above are due my deepest gratitude and thanks, as owing to them I was able to pursue this research and complete the dissertation.

Preface

This work is the published form of a dissertation submitted to the doctoral program in Arts and Science Education, at the Graduate School of Education of Hiroshima University. The dissertation was accepted, and I was accorded the degree of Doctor of Philosophy in Education in March, 2006.

Looking back upon the past, after already having worked as a junior high school teacher for six years I was given an opportunity by the Yamaguchi Prefectural Board of Education to study English language education in the master's course of the Graduate School of Education. The theoretical framework I acquired at the graduate school was very useful to me to link theory together with the experiences I had gained during the previous years as a teacher.

After graduating and returning to junior high school teaching, I continued on with my studies and research work, meanwhile doing occasional oral presentations and contributing articles to academic societies, including the Yamaguchi Association for English Language Education, the Chugoku Academic Society of English Language Education, and the Japan Society of English Language Education. During that time I received many insightful suggestions and comments from professionals in the field of education, and I entertained a hope to do further research work, backed up by more in-depth academic study.

Finally, this hope could be realized, as I was admitted to the doctoral program at the Graduate School of Education of Hiroshima University. From that time, besides teaching at the junior high school level, I pursued my doctoral research work encouraged on by many people. I highly value the experience of these three years, working both as a teacher and a researcher. In the end, I was able to complete my research and dissertation successfully.

Through the good offices of Mr. Kimura, the president of Keisuisha, Co., Ltd., it has now become possible to publish my dissertation, for which I wish to express my gratitude.

I hope this work will prove to be of benefit to teachers, academics, and others working in the field of English language education.

Yoko Fujiwara

A Study on the Acquisition of English Function-chains:
A Focus on Japanese EFL Learners

Chapter 1
Introduction

1.1 Background and purpose of the present study

The updated Course of Study, which came into effect from 2002 in Japan, introduced the concept of language use situations and functions[1] of language, and stated that students should be able to express themselves in a way appropriate[2] to the specific situation and condition. The English textbooks now in use were edited taking the concept of language use situations and functions of language into consideration. Still, this concept has yet to be fully applied to other aspects of the classroom environment, such as non-textbook teaching materials, classroom activities, and general interchanges between teachers and students. As Bardovi-Harlig (2001:31) argues, making conceptualized, pragmatically appropriate input available to learners from early stages of acquisition onward is the very least that pedagogy should aim to do. Providing realistic input in the classroom is necessary especially for EFL[3] learners with very little exposure to conversational English outside the classroom. Therefore, further research-based proposals for effective systematic programs for EFL settings are required. As part of that research the process by which Japanese EFL learners acquire the pragmatic competence to recognize appropriateness in the specific situations and social settings they might encounter needs to be investigated more deeply. The purpose of this thesis is to focus on that developmental process.

Appropriateness of language is considered to be one of the most important factors contributing to communicative competence. Niezgoda and Röver (2001:63-64) write that definitions of communicative competence tend to include (among other things) at least two components: a code component, which describes a language user's knowledge of syntax, morphology, semantics, lexis, and phonology; and a use component, which describes a language user's ability to use language appropriately for a purpose within a given context. Campbell and Wales (1970) and Hymes (1972) conceptualize communicative competence as the knowledge of rules of grammar, on the one hand, and rules of language use appropriate to a communicative situation, on the other. Based on their conceptualizations, detailed models of communicative competence have been suggested by Canale and Swain (1980, revised by Canale, 1983) and Bachman (1990, revised by Bachman & Palmer, 1996). Both models make a fundamental distinction between competencies for pragmatic aspects of language use and for aspects concerned with linguistic code features.

In the foreign language teaching context, curriculum development, teaching, and testing have traditionally focused on the aspects concerned with linguistic code features. But with the advent of communicative language teaching, attention has increasingly been paid to activities which promote the ability to interact appropriately in different situations. Such pragmatic aspects of language use lead us to consider language in terms of the communicative functions of sentences. Finocchiaro and Brumfit (1983:13) describe 'functions' in language use as communicative purposes which human beings wish to express at one time or another (e.g. apologizing, arguing, etc.). Others, such as Halliday (1973), Guntermann (1979), van Ek (1976), Papalia (1982), and Blundell et al. (1982), examined and put into lists the types of functions they considered appropriate for communicative course design. Cook (1991:47-48) goes further by pointing out the importance of seeing functions as inter-linked discourse moves[4]. The teacher using a communicative method should remember that functions never occur by themselves, but always in a sequence of conversational moves. Thus, this paper is concerned with the sequence of functions (what McCarthy (1991) calls "function-chains"), rather than a single utterance.

In conclusion, the author believes that the research dealing with appropriateness as regards function-chains will provide important insights into designing courses and materials which lead students towards greater fluency in their use of linguistic elements in communication.

1.2 Thesis outline

This dissertation is organized as follows:

Chapter 1 explains the background and the purpose of this research.

Chapter 2 reviews the literature in the field and the issues relevant to it, and explains the overall research design.

Chapter 3 highlights the results of the first study, which focused on beginning English learners (Japanese junior high school students) and their recognition of textual appropriateness in function-chains. In this study junior high school students were provided with only the function-chain structures in the test items (e.g.: Asking for reasons → Saying you do not know), and then asked to judge whether the structures were appropriate or not. The statistical analyses used are factor analysis and Hayashi's quantification model III.

Chapter 4 focuses on the second study. This study divided Japanese junior high school students into two groups (a relatively more advanced group and a less advanced group) according to their English proficiency level, and then investigated the relation between proficiency and pragmatic development, focusing on social and stylistic appropriateness. The statistical analysis used is a one-way layout multivariate analysis of variance (MANOVA)[5].

Chapter 5 presents the results of the third study (Analysis 1), which also focused on social and stylistic appropriateness. This study extended the range of participants and compared the following groups: Japanese junior high school students, Japanese university students, and native speakers from the United States. The Japanese university students were further sub-divided into a group of English major students with at least four months experience of study abroad, and a group of students who had majors other than English and lacked experience of study abroad. The statistical analysis used is a two-way layout analysis of variance (ANOVA)[6].

Chapter 6 summarizes the results of the third study (Analysis 2), comparing groups of Japanese students with native speakers from the United States, and then examining the characteristics specific to those Japanese students. As for analysis of data, a one-way layout ANOVA was used to obtain the quantitative results, and then a qualitative analysis was carried out. Matrices were used as a means of displaying, analyzing, and synthesizing the data in order to recognize any useful and informative patterns that might emerge.

Chapter 7 offers some concluding remarks, and it also presents some possible pedagogical implications for language teaching. Some remaining problems and implications for future research are also examined.

In summary, by evaluating and combining the results of these above mentioned studies, this thesis attempts to shed light on the process by which learners of English develop pragmatic competence as regards function-chains. In this way, the author hopes this thesis will make a useful contribution to English language teaching.

Notes

[1] function: the purpose for which an utterance or unit of language is used. In language teaching, language functions are often described as categories of behavior; e.g. requests, apologies, complaints, offers, compliments. The functional uses of language cannot be determined simply by studying the grammatical structure of sentences. For example, sentences in the imperative form may perform a variety of different functions:
    Give me that book. (Order)
    Pass the jam. (Request)
    Try the smoked salmon. (Suggestion)
    Come around on Sunday. (Invitation)
In linguistics, the functional uses of language are studied in speech act theory, sociolinguistics, and pragmatics. In the communicative approach to language teaching, a syllabus is often organized in terms of the different language functions the learner needs to express or understand. (Richards and Schmidt, 2002)

[2] appropriate: the extent to which a use of language matches the linguistic and sociolinguistic expectations and practices of native speakers of the language. When producing an utterance, a speaker needs to know that it is grammatical, and also that it is suitable (appropriate) for the particular situation. (Richards and Schmidt, 2002)

According to Corder (1973), the concept of appropriateness can be categorized into the following four areas: 1) referential appropriateness (which concerns whether there is an appropriate relationship between words and the things, actions, events, and qualities they stand for); 2) textual appropriateness (which concerns whether pairs of conversational utterances are appropriately sequenced); 3) social appropriateness (which concerns whether the utterance is appropriate to the social relationship of the speakers); and 4) stylistic appropriateness (which concerns whether the utterance is appropriate to the situation, the topic, the addressee(s) and the location). Thus, an utterance which meets these requirements is deemed appropriate. On the other hand, if it does not meet the sociolinguistic expectations of the situation, the utterance is deemed inappropriate, even when it is grammatically correct and an honest expression of the speaker's thoughts.

[3] EFL: an abbreviation for "English as a Foreign Language." Someone who learns English in a formal classroom setting, with limited or no opportunities for use outside the classroom, in a country in which English does not play an important role in internal communication (China, Japan, and Korea, for example), is said to be learning English as a foreign language. (Richards and Schmidt, 2002)

[4] discourse moves: Cook (1991) states that "discourse moves" refers to the speaker's choice of what to do in the conversation, e.g., opening moves such as a 'greeting'. There are certain opening moves for the conversation that can be chosen, then a choice of follow-up moves, a further choice of conversational moves linked to these, and so on, until the final exchange that ends the conversation.

[5] multivariate analysis of variance (MANOVA): a multivariate extension of univariate ANOVA to experimental situations where there are multiple dependent variables. (Richards and Schmidt, 2002)

[6] analysis of variance (ANOVA): a statistical procedure for testing whether the difference among the means of two or more groups is significant, for example, to compare the effectiveness of a teaching method on three different age groups. (Richards and Schmidt, 2002)

Chapter 2
Literature review

2.1 Historical perspective

2.1.1 Interlanguage[1] pragmatics in SLA[2]

This thesis focuses on the developmental process by which Japanese EFL learners acquire the pragmatic competence to recognize appropriateness as regards function-chains. The pragmatics of language learners are dealt with in interlanguage pragmatics studies. As early as 1991, Kasper and Dahl (1991:216) defined interlanguage pragmatics as referring to non-native speakers' comprehension and production of speech acts[3], and how that L2[4] -related knowledge is acquired.

Thus the definition offered by Kasper and Dahl included acquisition. However, as Kasper (1992:204) observes, the majority of interlanguage pragmatics studies focus on use, without much attempt to say or even imply anything about development. At the time that Kasper's (1992) article was written, relatively few longitudinal and cross-sectional studies[5] of interlanguage pragmatic development had been carried out. Longitudinal studies at that time included Schmidt's (1983) report on an adult Japanese learner of English, Schmidt and Frota's (1986) study of a beginning learner of Brazilian Portuguese, and Billmyer's (1990) study of instructed learners of English. Among the studies which employed a cross-sectional design were those of Scarcella (1979), Olshtain and Blum-Kulka (1985), Blum-Kulka and Olshtain (1986), Takahashi and Beebe (1987), Trosborg (1987), S. Takahashi and DuFon (1989), and Omar (1991).

7

Many longitudinal studies were published about the same time as Kasper's article, reflecting the fact that other researchers also saw the need for acquisitional research. These studies included Ellis's (1992) longitudinal study of two children's untutored acquisition of English requests, and Sawyer's (1992) study on the acquisition of the sentence-final particle *ne* by American learners of Japanese. Bouton (1992) investigated the development of comprehension as related to implicature, and Bardovi-Harlig and Hartford (1993) studied the changes in the speech acts of advanced non-native speakers.

After the rush of longitudinal studies around 1992, additional cross-sectional (Kerekes, 1992; Robinson, 1992; Svanes, 1992; Trosborg, 1995) and longitudinal (Siegal, 1994) studies were conducted. However, the relative handful of longitudinal, or even cross-sectional studies, had done very little to change the overall character of interlanguage pragmatics — the comparative stance of most studies, comparing what learners or non-native speakers do to what native speakers do.

At that time, Kasper and Schmidt (1996) repeated the observation that interlanguage pragmatics was more comparative than acquisitional. They pointed out that while other areas of L2 study are primarily concerned with acquisitional patterns of interlanguage knowledge over time, the great majority of studies in interlanguage pragmatics have focused on the ways non-native speakers' pragmalinguistic and sociopragmatic knowledge[6] differs from that of native speakers and among learners with different linguistic and cultural backgrounds. Therefore, interlanguage pragmatics has been primarily a study of L2 use rather than L2 learning.

But recently there have been a number of attempts to move interlanguage pragmatics closer to the mainstream of the SLA field. For example, Bardovi-Harlig (1999) assesses the state of acquisition research in interlanguage pragmatics, and shows how acquisition studies in interlanguage pragmatics differ from most of the studies conducted previously. Rose (2000) points out that the majority of interlanguage pragmatics research has examined pragmatic performance, not development, and states that garnering more attention for this underrepresented area is a welcome and much needed move. Kasper and Rose (2001) argue that most of the interlanguage research informs about learners' pragmatic ability at a particular point in time without relating it systematically. Joining the current of those favoring an acquisitional stance in pragmatics studies, this thesis focuses on interlanguage pragmatics from a developmental perspective that will tie it more closely to other areas of SLA.

2.1.2 Level of proficiency and pragmatic competence

As we have seen in the previous section (2.1.1), many articles from 1979 to 1996 have a tendency to identify non-native speakers as "non-native speakers" rather than learners. Rose (2000:34) notes that researchers have tended to rely on single-moment studies[7], and even in studies that employ a cross-sectional design, to treat groups of participants at various proficiency levels as a single group of non-native speakers in comparison with native speakers. According to Rose, such studies (e.g. Blum-Kulka and Olshtain (1986), Takahashi and Beebe (1987), Omar (1991) etc.) are capable of providing information regarding interlanguage pragmatic performance, but they say virtually nothing about development. Unlike performance research, studying pragmatic development requires an acquisitional study across time (in a longitudinal study), or across proficiency levels (in a cross-sectional study).

A consequence of the comparative focus of interlanguage pragmatics is that there have not been enough longitudinal studies to allow comparison across learners, contexts, or languages. However, there have been sufficient cross-sectional studies to begin to compare effects of levels of proficiency on pragmatic development.

In this section, we shall review existing cross-sectional studies that have researched the effects of level of proficiency.

Scarcella (1979) found that when making requests, the low-level students invariably relied on imperatives, whereas high-level learners showed sensitivity to status, using them only with equals and subordinates of one's immediate social circle.

Trosborg (1987) used role plays to compare the apologies of native speakers of English, native speakers of Danish, and three levels of Danish non-native speakers of English: intermediate, lower-advanced, and higher-advanced. She found that use of modality markers (e.g., downtoners, hedges, intensifiers) increased with proficiency across non-native speaker groups to a level closer to that of native speakers.

In another role-play study, Trosborg (1995) examined the requests, complaints, and apologies of three groups of Danish learners of English: secondary school grade 9, high school and commercial school, and university students. No proficiency tests were administered, but it was assumed that the three educational levels also represented proficiency levels. It was found that there was a closer approximation of native-like request strategies with increased proficiency, which included higher frequencies of adjuncts to main strategies (e.g., upgraders, downgraders, supportive moves[8]).

Maeshiba, Yoshinaga, Kasper, and Ross (1996) conducted a questionnaire study of apologies by intermediate and advanced Japanese learners of English, and reported that advanced learners were found to be better than intermediate learners at identifying contexts in which L1[9] apology strategies could and could not be used.

These studies suggest that with increasing L2 proficiency, pragmatic competence may develop. However, other areas have been found in which proficiency level appears to have less impact on the development of pragmatic competence. For example, Takahashi (1996) examined the requests of low- and high- proficiency Japanese university students, and found only minimal proficiency effects on learners' transferability perceptions. Both groups relied equally on L1 request conventions. In the above mentioned study of Trosborg (1995), only slight differences were obtained across groups as regards principal apology and complaint strategies, with a higher incidence of opting out among the lower proficiency groups. As Kasper (1999)[10] points out, the absence of a proficiency effect may be due to the fact that real beginners were not included in the studies. Kasper and Schmidt (1996.151) also state that one drawback in the design of the pseudolongitudinal studies is that none of them involves subjects at the very first stages of interlanguage development. Some studies include only intermediate and advanced learners, and studies in which the lowest proficiency group is labeled "beginners" often refer to learners whose command of the target language is good enough to fill in a discourse completion questionnaire or engage in a role-play. Kasper (1992) states that our elicitation[11] tasks favor advanced learners, and the availability of English-speaking undergraduate and graduate students at universities around the world has reinforced the tendency to use advanced learners rather than learners at all levels. This is one of the reasons why interlanguage pragmatics has developed with the comparative stance of non-native speakers to native speakers, with little attempt to investigate different stages of pragmatic development in detail. However, a study which involves beginning-level learners would likely uncover the early developmental patterns in interlanguage pragmatic knowledge. Therefore, this thesis expands learner populations to include beginning English learners (Japanese junior high school students), and investigates the early stages of pragmatic development.

2.1.3 Types of function-chains and pragmatic competence

As we have seen, the field of research into interlanguage pragmatics has proliferated since the early 1980s. A considerable amount of research has been undertaken into a variety of language functions — requests (e.g., Scarcella, 1979; Blum-Kulka and Olshtain, 1986; Takahashi and DuFon, 1989; Ellis, 1992; Takahashi, 2001; Fukazawa, 2003), apologies (e.g., Olshtain and Cohen, 1983; Trosborg, 1987; Maeshiba, Yoshinaga, Kasper and Ross, 1996), refusals (e.g., Takahashi and Beebe, 1987; Robinson, 1992), complaints (e.g., Murphy and Neu, 1996), offering advice (e.g., Matsumura, 2001, 2003), compliments and compliment responses (e.g., Holmes and Brown, 1987; Billmyer, 1990a, 1990b), among others. Some research deals with multiple speech acts within the same study — suggestions and rejections (Bardovi-Harlig and Hartford, 1993), assertiveness and supportiveness (Kerekes, 1992), requests, complaints, and apologies (Trosborg, 1995), requests, apologies, and compliments (Rose, 2000), five initiating speech acts (requests, suggestions, offers, invitations, complaints) and six responding speech acts (acceptance, promises, objections, rejections, apologies, thanks) (Kasper, 1981), among others.

These studies have revealed a number of patterns in pragmatic performance or development — how native speakers and non-native speakers differ in their use of pragmatic knowledge in production and comprehension, or how pragmatic competence develops across time. In both of these cases, many studies have examined learners' command of particular language functions, focusing on requests, apologies, compliment responses and so on. But relative comparison among those types of functions is another area requiring more research.

For example, Blum-Kulka and Olshtain (1986) noted that learners' use of supportive moves in request performance followed a bell-shaped developmental curve, starting out with an underuse of supportive moves, followed by an overuse, and finally a level of use approximating a target-like distribution. This pattern reflected increasing L2 proficiency. What we are concerned with here is whether such a developmental curve varies depending on the type of function involved — that is to say, whether each type of function shows its own unique rate and route of development for certain learners.

A further point which needs to be asked is whether, for certain learners, the different types of functions present distinctly different levels of difficulty or not. Namely, this is a question regarding the relative level of difficulty of the types of functions.

It is true that in-depth studies with a focus on particular language functions have proven fruitful in illuminating certain aspects of interlanguage pragmatic development. At the same time, relative comparison among those types of functions may provide further insights and information of value regarding learners' overall developmental process. Thus, in this thesis, we deal with various types of functions as one of the variables to explain learners' interlanguage pragmatics, and examine the structures and relations between the types of function-chains.

2.2 Sociolinguistic perspective

This thesis focuses attention on the ability to use appropriate language while communicating and interacting with others. Using language appropriately helps to improve communication. On the other hand, using it inappropriately can have the opposite effect. Therefore, it is important to choose the manner of expression suitable for each occasion. This brings us to the question of how we decide what kind of language to use in a variety of real-world situations, that is, what concepts influence the way in which we express ourselves. In this section we will review the theoretical bases, and discuss what determines appropriateness.

When communication takes place there is always a communicative purpose involved, that is, what people want to do or what they want to accomplish through speech. It is functionally organized: e.g., agreeing, refusing, offering, apologizing, expressing hopes, fears, and so on. While the functions to be expressed depend solely on the purpose(s) of the speaker, the language we actually produce (i.e., exponent) changes according to what situation we are in. Finocchiaro and Brumfit (1983:15-16) state that a situation includes 1) the persons, 2) the place, 3) the time, and 4) the topic or activity.

According to Finocchiaro and Brumfit, as regards the persons taking part in the speech act, we need to take into consideration the following factors: their age, sex, the language, languages, or dialects they are using, the number of the people, their social roles and status in the community, and their attitudes toward each other (e.g., friends, enemies, strangers, acquaintances).

The place where the conversation occurs is also an important factor: whether it is in the speaker's native land or in a foreign country; and whether it is in a house, an office, a place of worship, a movie, or a park. The place determines whether the speech act must be brief, spoken in a whisper, or in a normal voice.

As for the time it takes place, we should consider whether it is a usual daily occurrence, whether it is a frequent or infrequent happening, the duration of the conversation, and whether it is time-bound or time-free, e.g., "Good evening" or "Hello."

Our psychological attitude and manner of expression will also differ depending on the topic or activity which is being discussed. For example, whether it is an important business deal or a pleasant social conversation will change our linguistic realization. Finocchiaro and Brumfit observe that different communicative purposes and situations lead us to adapt our messages so that they will be most clearly understood. When we use language we are constantly adapting and adjusting our messages. Their work provides the following examples of making a suggestion using different levels of formality: "How about (or What about) coming to the movies tonight?" (casual, colloquial or familiar style); "Would you like to come to the movies tonight?" (informal style); "Do you think there is a good film we might go to see tonight?" (consultative style); "Might I escort you to the movies tonight?" (formal style); and "I would deem it a privilege if you would accompany me to the cinema tonight." (frozen style, which could only be used in this context as a joke.) Richards and Schmidt (2002) explain the phenomenon by which style varies from casual to formal as "style shift."

In this way, communicative behavior is situationally conditioned. Finocchiaro and Brumfit also mention that the exponents we select in speaking depend not only on the situational elements above but on our personalities, educational background, and level of linguistic competence. Additionally, their work takes into consideration the influence of pre-suppositions (the shared sociocultural allusions). In regards to pre-suppositions, they deal with paralinguistic features of languages, such as tone of voice, groans, sighs, and other unarticulated sounds which convey meaning to a listener, and kinesics, such as gestures, facial expressions, and physical distance between the speakers. Parts of messages in communication might be misunderstood or given false values in the case that these elements are not shared by the listener and speaker. Therefore, we can say that the shared sociocultural allusions are not only necessary to a complete understanding of the messages we receive, but also determine their acceptability or appropriateness.

Thus Finocchiaro and Brumfit discuss appropriateness as an expression of sociolinguistic factors. If we schematize their explanation about this point, the diagram would look something like this (see Figure 1):

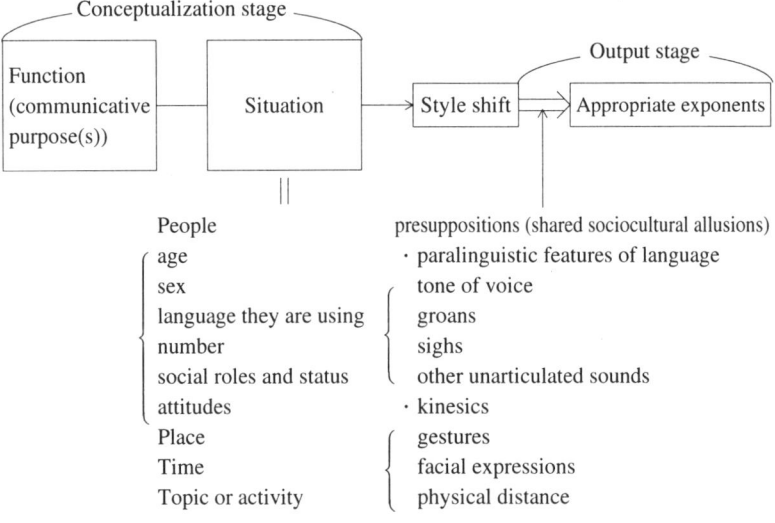

Figure 1. **Factors influencing appropriateness**

After going through these steps, we produce appropriate exponents. We should take into consideration the same steps when judging the appropriateness of the exponents as well. Especially, as Scollon and Scollon (2001:59) point out, the calculation of the appropriate level of face strategies is always inextricably tied to the expression of the hierarchical system of relationship between or among the participants. Therefore, many researchers have presented scenarios to their respondents including a variety of status relationships when carrying out appropriateness judgment tests (e.g., Matsumura, 2001, 2003).

Blundell, Higgens, and Middlemiss (1982), the comprehensive work to classify the English language in functional terms, is of value for reference, because it considers the concept of function, exponents, and style shift. It describes 140 functions using over 3,000 exponents. These exponents are in turn classified according to three levels of formality: neutral, informal, and formal. In this thesis, therefore, the list of Blundell, Higgens, and Middlemiss (1982) was the basic source used to categorize the test items.

2.3 Conclusions from the literature review and overall research design

In this chapter, we have reviewed the literature dealing with the ability to use language appropriate to a communicative situation from a historical and sociolinguistic perspective.

From this review the following three insights can be gleaned.

First, as those favoring an acquisitional stance in pragmatics studies have pointed out, the process of development by which L2 learners acquire pragmatic knowledge should be investigated more deeply.

Second, previous studies have largely overlooked beginning-level learners. Therefore, such a study, which may help to uncover the early developmental patterns in interlanguage pragmatic knowledge, is advisable.

Third, it is important to see functions as inter-linked discourse moves. Attention should be focused on the sequence of functions (function-chains) rather than a single utterance. When studying function-chains, relative comparison among the types of function-chains should provide some information of value regarding learners' overall developmental process.

Based on these insights, the present research addresses the following research questions (RQ):

RQ1: What kind of relationships can be seen between the function-chains used as the test items in this study? And also what is the relation between the patterns found and the junior high school students' judgment as regards textual appropriateness? (→ Study 1)

RQ2: How does the level of proficiency in English and the type of function-chains employed affect the ability of students to recognize social and stylistic appropriateness? (→ Study 2 and Study 3 [Analyses 1 and 2])

First, to answer RQ1, Japanese junior high school students (beginning English learners) were provided with only the function-chain structures in the test items (e.g.: Asking for reasons → Saying you do not know), and then were asked to judge whether the structures were appropriate or not. Factor analysis and Hayashi's quantification model III were applied to the results of the appropriateness judgment test.

Next, to address RQ2, two studies (Studies 2 and 3) were conducted. In Study 1, the students were provided with only the function-chain structures in the test items. In Studies 2 and 3, for each test item the setting, the social relationship of the addresser and the addressee, and actual utterances were provided, as well as the function-chain structures. Study 2 divided Japanese junior high school students into two groups (a relatively high proficiency group and a low proficiency group), and then investigated the relation between proficiency and pragmatic development. In order to analyze the obtained data, a one-way layout MANOVA was conducted. Study 3 extended the range of participants to Japanese university students and native speakers from the United States, and then investigated the route of development as regards recognition of appropriateness for the function-chains. The statistical analysis used in Analysis 1 was a two-way layout ANOVA. Further, in Analysis 2, a one-way layout ANOVA was applied to the data obtained in Analysis 1. Qualitative analysis was employed, along with the quantitative results from the one-way layout ANOVA.

In the following chapters, the details of the four analyses dealing with function-chains will be looked at. As will be seen, the results of these analyses help to clarify the process by which Japanese learners acquire the pragmatic competence to recognize what constitutes appropriate expressions of English in various real-life situations.

Notes

[1] interlanguage: the type of language produced by second- and foreign-language learners who are in the process of learning a language. In language learning, learner language is influenced by several different processes. These include:
a) borrowing patterns from the mother tongue;
b) extending patterns from the target language, e.g., by analogy;
c) expressing meanings using the words and grammar which are already known.

Since the language which the learner produces using these processes differs from both the mother tongue and the target language, it is sometimes called an interlanguage, or is said to result from the learner's interlanguage system or approximative system. (Richards and Schmidt, 2002)

[2] SLA: an acronym for Second Language Acquisition. The process of acquiring a second or foreign language. (Richards and Schmidt, 2002)

[3] speech act: an utterance as a functional unit in communication. In speech act theory, utterances have two kinds of meanings:
a) propositional meaning (also known as locutionary meaning). This is the basic literal meaning of the utterance which is conveyed by the particular words and structures which the utterance contains.
b) illocutionary meaning (also known as illocutionary force). This is the effect the

utterance or written text has on the reader or listener.

For example, in *I am thirsty* the propositional meaning is what the utterance says about the speaker's physical state. The illocutionary force is the effect the speaker wants the utterance to have on the listener. It may be intended as a request for something to drink. A speech act is a sentence or utterance which has both propositional meaning and illocutionary force. There are many different kinds of speech acts, such as the speech act of requesting above. Indirect speech acts are often felt to be more polite ways of performing certain kinds of speech acts, such as requests and refusals. In language teaching, and syllabus design, speech acts are often referred to as "functions" or "language functions." (Richards and Schmidt, 2002)

[4] L2: another term for a target language or second language. (Richards and Schmidt, 2002)

[5] longitudinal and cross-sectional studies: a cross-sectional study is a study of a group of different individuals or subjects at a single point in time, in order to measure or study a particular topic or aspect of language (for example, use of the tense system of a language). This can be contrasted with a longitudinal method or longitudinal study, in which an individual or group is studied over a period of time (for example, to study how the use of the tense system changes and develops with age.). (Richards and Schmidt, 2002)

[6] pragmalinguistic and sociopragmatic knowledge: pragmalinguistics is the interface between linguistics and pragmatics, focusing on the linguistic means used to accomplish pragmatic ends. For example, when a learner asks "How do I make a compliment (or a request, or a warning) in this language?", this is a question of pragmalinguistics knowledge. This can be contrasted with sociopragmatics and sociopragmatic knowledge, which concern the relationship between social factors and pragmatics. For example, a learner might need to know in what circumstances it is appropriate to make a compliment in the target language, and which form would be most appropriate given the social relationship between speaker and listener. (Richards and Schmidt, 2002)

[7] single-moment studies: a cross-sectional study looks at different learners at different moments in time and establishes development by comparing these successive states in different people. Other studies do not compare groups of learners at different cross-sectional levels to establish a series of developmental language states, but either lump all the learners together in one group, or separate them by first language or criteria other than chronological development. A further term, *single-moment studies*, has sometimes been used to distinguish this approach from the true cross-sectional design. (Cook, 1993)

[8] supportive moves: clauses or sentences external to the main request which either mitigate or aggravate the force of a request. Blum-Kulka, House, and Kasper (1989: 287-289) offer a coding manual for supportive moves as follows: Preparator (e.g., *I'd like to ask you something...*), Getting a precommitment (e.g., *Could you do me a favor?*), Grounder (e.g., Judith, *I missed class yesterday.* Could I borrow your notes?), Disarmer (e.g., *I know you don't like lending out your notes*, but could you make an exception this time?), Promise of reward (e.g., Could you give me a lift home? *I'll pitch in on some gas.*), Imposition minimizer (e.g., Would you give me a lift, *but only if you're going my way.*). There are aggravating, as well as mitigating, supportive moves, such as threats (e.g., Move that car *if you don't want a ticket!*). In request realizations, combinations of these moves are sometimes used in order to modify the head act. (Fukazawa and Sasaki, 2004)

[9] L1: (generally) a person's mother tongue or the language acquired first. In multilingual communities, however, where a child may gradually shift from the main use of one language to the main use of another (e.g., because of the influence of a school language), first language may refer to the language the child feels most comfortable using. Often this term is used synonymously with native language. (Richards and Schmidt, 2002)

[10] This was Kasper's comment to Bardovi-Harlig based on a personal communication they had in March 1999. (Bardovi-Harlig, 1999)

[11] elicitation: any technique or procedure that is designed to get a person to actively produce speech or writing, for example, asking someone to describe a picture, tell a story, or finish an incomplete sentence. In linguistics, these techniques are used to prompt native speakers to produce linguistic data for analysis. In teaching and second language research, the same and similar techniques are used to get a better picture of learner abilities, or a fuller understanding of interlanguage than the study of naturally occurring speech or writing can provide. (Richards and Schmidt, 2002)

Chapter 3
Study 1: Junior high students' recognition of the appropriateness of function-chain structures

3.1 Objectives

This study attempts to reveal the relationships between the function-chains used as the test items, and also the relation between the patterns found and the junior high school students' judgment as regards textual appropriateness. The following research questions are the foci of this study.
(1) What kind of factors can be extracted to explain the relation between the function-chains and the students' judgment?
(2) Are there any differences in junior high school students' judgment of appropriateness between the function-chains from a series of authorized junior high school English textbooks and the function-chains from a corpus of scripted speech?

3.2 Method

3.2.1 Participants

The participants in this study were 69 third year junior high school students in Yamaguchi Prefecture in Japan.

3.2.2 Materials

The author extracted function-chains from a series of authorized junior high school English textbooks (*NEW HORIZON English Course*), and also from the script of a BBC broadcast, and then made a list (see Figure 2). When classifying the functions, the categories used in Blundell, Higgens and Middlemiss (1982) were the ones used in most cases[1].

	Actual Utterance	Function
First speaker (Stimulus)	Is it really safe?	13 (= Asking if someone is sure about something)
Second speaker (Response)	Yes, of course.	14 (= Saying you are sure)

Figure 2. An example of a function-chain pattern:
function 13 to function 14

The function number 13 and 14 in Figure 2 are from the *List of functions* in Blundell, Higgens, and Middlemiss (1982). Figure 2 shows one communication pattern: the first speaker says "Is it really safe?" and the second speaker replies, "Yes, of course." When we use functions, the pattern can be shown like this: <u>Stimulus: Asking if someone is sure about something.</u> → <u>Response: Saying you are sure.</u> This is one example of how function-chain patterns from the English textbooks and a sample of scripted speech were extracted and used in the test items.

3.2.3 Procedure

The test items were selected from the function-chains extracted so as to include at least one sample of scripted speech and one sample of a stimulus with several alternative responses (see Appendix A). The reasons for this were 1) to investigate the students' judgment as regards appropriateness of the patterns from scripted speech, and 2) to investigate the different responses to the same stimulus. A sample of the questions follows.

Table 1. An example from the test items

Please write ○ if you think the conversational patterns are appropriately sequenced, and write × if you think the sequence is inappropriate (unnatural).
(A) Saying you are pessimistic (Saying you are worried or afraid)
   1. Asking for reasons (Trying to change someone's opinion (including arguing back))
   2. Saying you are bored (Being sarcastic about something)

For example, when the first speaker uses the pattern Saying you are pessimistic (Saying you are worried or afraid), two response patterns 1. Asking for reasons (Trying to change someone's opinion (including arguing back)) and 2. Saying you are bored (Being sarcastic about something) were found, giving two possible function-chains: A1 and A2. The letters A−S are used to represent the 19 different stimuli used in the test, and numbers to represent responses. The students judged each 19 function-chains as appropriate or not. In order to investigate whether the students have metalinguistic knowledge[2] or not, only the functions and the Japanese translation of them were given, and no actual utterances were given to the participants. In other words, this study focused on the students' recognition of textual appropriateness in function-chains.

Before the test, the author gave the students a supplementary explanation in Japanese. The explanation was as follows: "In conversation, we can see some patterns. For example, when someone says "Good morning" to you, you also say "Good morning" to him or her. This is a Greeting − Greeting pattern. Then, how about the following interactions? Please write ○ if you think the conversational patterns are appropriately sequenced, and write × if you think the sequence is inappropriate." There were 71 questions in all (Patterns A1 − S7), but a printing error in S4 reduced the number to 70, of which 40 came from the English textbooks and 30 from the scripted speech. In this study, all the test items (the patterns of function-chains) were appropriately sequenced, and thus the number of items answered as ○ corresponded to the number of correct answers.

3.3 Results

3.3.1 Results of factor analysis

The author applied factor analysis to the results of the function-chain test. Here, the author combined items A1 and A2 as Section A, and items S1 to S7 as Section S. The factor analysis was used to interpret the features of each section (Sections A − S). The data to be discussed below was collected in the following way.

First, the author calculated the percentage of correct answers in each section (Sections A − S). These percentages represented the ease of response in each section. Based on the percentage of correct answers to each section (19) × participants (69) matrix, three factors were extracted in order of importance to explain the features of all the sections (Sections A − S) by principal component method. Furthermore, factor rotation by the varimax method was used. The contributions of the three factors (Factor 1, Factor 2, and Factor 3) finally extracted were 13.427%, 9.472%, and 8.447% respectively, and the cumulative contribution was 31.345%. Then the factor loading (the correlation between each function-chain [Section A − S] and each factor) was calculated.

The cumulative contribution found here was a little over 30%, therefore, its value is not large enough to explain the variance of participants' scores. Even so, it may be going too far to disregard the relatively weak contribution in this area. Hence, although the interpretation of each factor might be tentative, it is important to continue the analysis in an attempt to reach a hypothesis which would permit further study. Therefore, the author would like to interpret the three factors based on the factor loadings.

Table 2. Function-chains with large factor loadings in Factor 1

Section O (O) Asking about likes
    1. Expressing likes
    2. Expressing dislikes
    3. Expressing likes (Acknowledging something for the present)
    4. Suggesting
    5. Saying you remember — Saying what you prefer

Section P (P) Giving your opinion
    1. Saying you partly agree (Comparing)
    2. Saying something is correct
    3. Agreeing
    4. Trying to change someone's opinion
    5. Turning something into a joke

Section R (R) Asking for reasons
    1. Saying you do not know
    2. Giving reasons
    3. Giving reasons (Covering up a fact)
    4. Inviting someone
    5. Justifying oneself
    6. Asking back

Section S (S) Trying to change someone's opinion (including arguing back)
    1. Calming or reassuring someone
    2. Saying you partly agree
    3. Trying to change someone's opinion (including arguing back) (Talking about what might happen)
    4. Justifying oneself
    5. Making an excuse (including explaining the details)
    6. Saying you intend to do something

Table 3. Function-chains with large factor loadings in Factor 2

Section F (F) Expressing surprise
    1. Identifying/Reporting
    2. Saying you are curious (Asking for information)
    3. Saying something is correct
Section G (G) Saying you are excited
    1. Reporting
    2. Saying you are disappointed
    3. Saying you are excited

Table 4. Function-chains with large factor loadings in Factor 3

Section J (J) Saying you are displeased or angry
    1. Saying you are worried or afraid (Talking about what might happen)
    2. Saying sorry
    3. Saying you approve
    4. Showing you are listening
Section M (M) Blaming someone
    1. Saying sorry
    2. Calming or reassuring someone
    3. Giving yourself time to think — Saying someone must not do something
    4. Giving yourself time to think — Making an excuse (including explaining the details)

As for Factor 1, the eigenvalue was 2.551. Sections O, P, R, and S had large loadings in Factor 1, which were −0.547, −0.606, −0.568, and −0.530 respectively.

The common feature of these function-chains is asking or giving one's opinion (see Table 2).

As for Factor 2, the eigenvalue was 1.800. Sections F and G had large loadings in Factor 2, which were −0.595 and − 0.517 respectively.

The common feature of these function-chains is expressing surprise or excitement (see Table 3).

As for Factor 3, the eigenvalue was 1.605. Sections J and M had large loadings in Factor 3, which were 0.569 and 0.666 respectively.

The common feature of these function-chains is expressing displeasure at a situation or an utterance (see Table 4).

However, we observe some function-chains whose factor loadings were very close to the loadings of some sections in Tables 2, 3, and 4, and which cannot be explained by Factors 1, 2, and 3. Thus, the reliability of the features of these factors is not high.

3.3.2 Results of Hayashi's quantification model III

Next, on the 70 function-chains in Sections A − S and for each participant, the author indicated the correct answers by 1 and the incorrect answers by 0. Then the author applied Hayashi's quantification model III to the results and obtained two dimensions (Dimension I and Dimension II). In other words, the author tried to evaluate the students' judgment according to their choice of either 1 or 0 for each function-chain, and then converting the students' results into two scores (1 and 0) to which were applied Hayashi's quantification model III. This was the process by which the structure of the 70 function-chains was analyzed. The eigenvalue of Dimension I was 0.076, and the eigenvalue of Dimension II was 0.048. The eigenvalue corresponds to the square of the coefficient of correlation. Therefore, the eigenvalue of Dimension I corresponds to a correlation coefficient of about 0.276 (the square root of 7.6%). This score of 0.276 shows that there was a weak correlation between the 70 function-chains and the participants included in Dimension I. Similarly, the eigenvalue of Dimension II corresponds to a correlation coefficient of about 0.219 (the square root of 4.8%). This score of 0.219 signifies that there was a weak correlation between the 70 function-chains and the participants included in Dimension II. The eigenvalues of Dimension I and Dimension II do not seem to be high enough to explain the variance in the participants' judgment and thus the interpretation made of each dimension's results might be

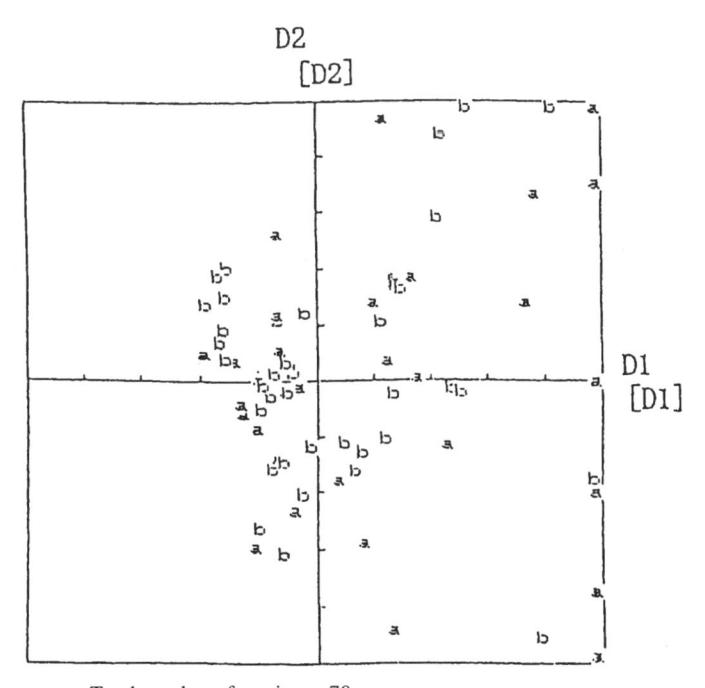

Total number of test items: 70
X-axis: Dimension I / Y-axis: Dimension II
a: The items from the scripted speech ($N = 30$)
b: The items from the English textbooks ($N = 40$)

Figure 3. The location of each function-chain on the coordinate (X-axis: Dimension I, Y-axis: Dimension II) by using Hayashi's quantification model III

tentative. However, it is important to continue with the analysis in an attempt to find a hypothesis for further study. Therefore, the author would like to go ahead with the interpretation of the dimensions based on the information we obtained.

Figure 3 shows 70 function-chains on the coordinate (X-axis: Dimension I, Y-axis: Dimension II). The dimensions correlate the participants and the function-chains. The category score shows the weight of each function-chain in each dimension. In Figure 3, the scale of the X-axis and the Y-axis ranges from $+2.5$ to -2.5. As for the dots beyond those values on the scale, their category scores are all represented as $+2.5$ or -2.5 as a matter of convenience. Figure 3 also shows the distinction in the results obtained between the function-chains from a corpus of scripted speech (a) and the function-chains from the English textbooks (b).

Table 5 shows the mean and the standard deviation (*SD*) of the category scores of each group (Group a: function-chains from a corpus of scripted speech, Group b: function-chains from the English textbooks) under Dimension I and Dimension II.

We see from Figure 3 and Table 5 that the *SD* of the category score

Table 5. The mean and the standard deviation of the category scores of each group under Dimension I and Dimension II

	Dimension I	Dimension II
[a: Function-chains from a sample of scripted speech]	$N = 30$ *Mean*: 0.911 *SD*: 1.877	-0.185 1.674
[b: Function-chains from English textbooks]	$N = 40$ *Mean*: 0.075 *SD*: 0.858	0.113 1.100

of Group a was large. The *SD* of the category score of Group b, on the other hand, was smaller than that of Group a.

Further, the scale of Figure 3 was extended to make the location of each dot clear, because the indication of the category score beyond $+2.5$ or -2.5 did not fit in Figure 3. The result of the extension of the scale is represented in Figure 4. In this figure, the scale of the X-axis is $+7$ to -2 and the scale of the Y-axis is from $+4$ to -8.

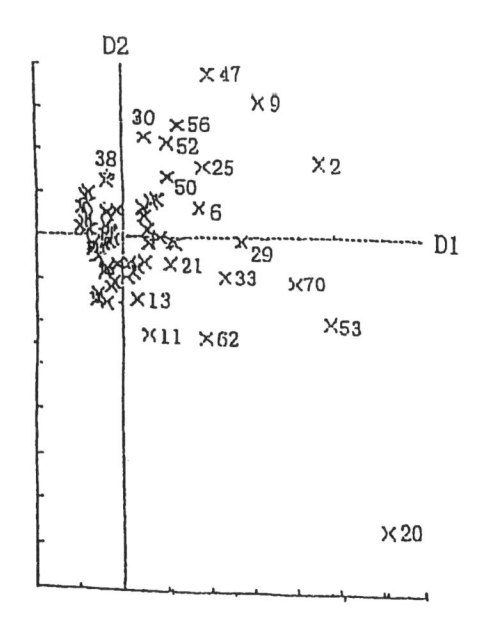

Total number of test items: 70
X-axis = Dimension I (D1) / Y-axis = Dimension II (D2)
Number added to each dot = Number of test item

Figure 4. The location of each function-chain on the coordinate (X-axis: Dimension I, Y-axis: Dimension II) by using Hayashi's quantification model III

Table 6. Category score of each test item (function-chain) by using Hayashi's quantification model III

Variable labels	Dimension I	Dimension II	Variable labels	Dimension I	Dimension II
Test item 1	− 0.220	− 0.077	Test item 38	− 0.403	1.279
2	4.570	1.726	39	− 0.180	− 1.045
3	0.616	0.841	40	− 0.342	− 0.747
4	− 0.559	− 0.023	41	1.123	− 0.105
5	− 0.868	0.424	42	− 0.163	0.586
6	1.759	0.686	43	− 0.587	− 0.446
7	− 0.116	− 0.622	44	− 0.427	0.035
8	− 0.399	− 0.725	45	− 0.353	− 1.574
9	3.183	3.150	46	− 0.306	0.117
10	− 0.708	− 0.313	47	2.008	3.846
11	0.605	− 2.237	48	0.439	0.681
12	− 0.263	0.049	49	− 0.332	0.127
13	0.347	− 1.465	50	1.006	1.409
14	0.595	− 0.151	51	− 0.855	0.167
15	0.268	− 0.835	52	1.032	2.159
16	− 0.467	− 0.165	53	4.834	− 1.906
17	− 1.010	0.660	54	− 0.561	− 1.331
18	0.120	− 0.917	55	0.493	0.496
19	− 0.724	− 0.234	56	1.256	2.653
20	6.142	− 6.536	57	1.205	− 0.131
21	1.084	− 0.606	58	− 0.599	− 1.505
22	− 1.031	0.209	59	0.659	0.791
23	0.167	− 0.585	60	− 0.544	− 0.278
24	− 0.907	0.322	61	− 0.846	0.733
25	1.843	1.637	62	1.893	− 2.297
26	− 0.390	0.245	63	0.558	0.145
27	− 0.829	0.974	64	0.824	0.003
28	− 0.323	− 0.136	65	0.330	− 0.670
29	2.749	− 0.032	66	− 0.536	− 0.068
30	0.509	2.319	67	− 0.920	0.912
31	− 0.402	0.523	68	− 0.247	− 1.184
32	− 0.537	− 0.302	69	− 0.403	0.562
33	2.362	− 0.911	70	4.038	− 1.034
34	− 0.772	0.144	Eigenvalue	0.076	0.048
35	0.525	− 0.552	Contribution (%)	9.765	6.201
36	− 0.443	− 0.815	Cumulative Contribution (%)	9.765	15.965
37	0.760	0.904			

The author found out what number of test items (1 − 70) corresponded to each dot by comparing the location of the dot with the category scores assigned to each test item (see Table 6). Then Dimension I and Dimension II were interpreted based on the features of the function-chains for which the category scores were high.

From Figure 3 and Table 6, the author concluded that the function-chains 20, 53, 2, and 70 had high category scores in Dimension I.

Table 7. Function-chains with high category scores in Dimension I

20	Stimulus: Being sarcastic about something
	→ Response: Greeting someone − Inviting someone
53	Stimulus: Giving your opinion
	→ Response: Turning something into a joke
2	Stimulus: Saying you are pessimistic (Saying you are worried or afraid)
	→ Response: Saying you are bored (Being sarcastic about something)
70	Stimulus: Trying to change someone's opinion (including arguing back)
	→ Response: Despising something (someone)

The common feature of these function-chains is satire and scorn.

As for the function-chains with high category scores in Dimension II, first of all note function-chain No.20 (Figure 4). If there were some more function-chains distributed around the dot No.20, we could interpret Dimension II taking into consideration the features of No.20. However, in actuality, it is difficult to interpret Dimension II by considering only the features of No.20. Therefore, the author instead interpreted Dimension II based on the features of the function-chains No.47 and No.9, for which the absolute values of the category scores were smaller than that of No.20, but the largest values apart from No.20.

Table 8. Function-chains with high category scores in Dimension II

47	Stimulus: Asking about likes → Response: Suggesting
9	Stimulus: Demeaning oneself → Response: Agreeing

In these function-chains, the responses were witty, not serious. (For example, in No.9, an expected response might be "calming or reassuring someone" or "disagreeing." But instead, the second speaker agrees with the first speaker, who has just spoken in disapproval of herself. It causes humor.)

It should be noted that as there was no hypothesis made beforehand, the reliability of the interpretation of these axes is not absolute.

3.4 Discussion

In this investigation, factor analysis was applied to the results of the junior high school students' judgment, and then the three factors were extracted which best explained the relation between the function-chains (Sections A − S) and the students' judgment. The author interpreted the three factors based on the factor loadings. In view of that interpretation, it may be possible to infer that Factor 1 means "asking or giving one's opinion," Factor 2 means "expressing surprise or excitement," and Factor 3 means "expressing displeasure." However, we should take further steps to check the reliability of this interpretation of these three factors. That is, we should pick out the items relevant to the factors and then analyze the judgment of the students once again.

Hayashi's quantification model III was also used, and the two dimensions (Dimension I and Dimension II) were extracted. The author interpreted Dimension I and Dimension II by the features of the function-chains whose category scores were high. According to that interpretation, we may say that Dimension I was the axis that meant "satire and scorn" and Dimension II was the axis that meant "inventiveness in communication." By plotting 70 function-chains, we were able to make clear the relationships among them. Then, we found that the standard deviation (*SD*) of the category score of the function-chains from a corpus of scripted speech was large. From this we may infer that various patterns or factors were involved in forming the junior high school students' judgment as regards the function-chains from the scripted speech. On the other hand, the variation of students' judgment concerning the function-chains from English textbooks was smaller than that from the scripted speech. That is, as a whole the junior high school students reached similar judgments on the function-chains from English textbooks. Hence, we can say that the students have different attitudes towards the function-chains from the scripted speech and the function-chains from English textbooks.

However, the author suggests that multivariate analysis with more appropriate data could be used as a method to yield more significant information. It is also necessary to examine the validity of the features interpreted in this research.

Notes

[1] When classifying the functions, the categories used in Blundell, Higgens and Middlemiss (1982) were basically referred to. Among the functions used as the test items, the following were developed because they did not come under the categories in Blundell, Higgens and Middlemiss: Asking for reasons, Arguing back, Being sarcastic about something, Demeaning oneself, Making an excuse (including explaining the details), Saying you understand, Calling someone's name, Turning something into a joke, Blaming someone, Asking back, Acknowledging something for the present,

Saying how you feel after something has happened, Covering up a fact, Justifying oneself, and Despising something (someone). As for Identifying, Reporting, and Denying something, which are not included in Blundell, Higgens, and Middlemiss, the author referred to van Ek (1976).

[2] metalinguistic knowledge: (in language learning) knowledge of the forms, structure and other aspects of a language, which a learner arrives at through reflecting on and analyzing the language. In linguistic analysis, researchers sometimes make use of a native speaker's metalinguistic knowledge as one source of information about the language. (Richards and Schmidt, 2002)

Chapter 4
Study 2: The recognition of the appropriateness of actual utterances by junior high students at two proficiency levels

4.1 Objectives

In the previous chapter, the author revealed the relationships between the function-chains used as the test items, and also the relation between the patterns found and junior high school students' judgment as regards textual appropriateness. The participants were junior high school students, and their recognition of appropriateness as regards function-chains was researched.

The present study divides junior high school students into two groups according to the level of proficiency in English, and then investigates the relation between proficiency and pragmatic development. The following are the research questions in this study.

(1) Do the students with high English proficiency achieve higher levels of recognition of appropriateness as regards function-chains?

(2) What kinds of function-chains, if any, show a significant difference in difficulty between the high proficiency and low proficiency groups?

These questions will offer the fundamental information on the process by which beginning English learners develop pragmatic competence as regards function-chains.

4.2 Method

4.2.1 Participants and determination of their level of proficiency in English

The participants in the study were 150 third year junior high school students in Hiroshima Prefecture in Japan. Sixty grammar questions from a past Test of Practical English[1] were selected, with 20 questions being taken from the 4th, 3rd, and pre-2nd grade tests respectively (see Appendix B). The students took the test and were divided into two groups according to the median[2] score of 40 points (60 points maximum). The mean of the relatively high proficiency group (76 students) was 45.80 and the standard deviation (SD) was 4.915. The mean of the low proficiency group (74 students) was 29.86 and the SD was 6.411. There was a significant difference between the two groups (t (148) $= -17.114, p < .001$). The Cronbach's alpha (reliability rating) of this proficiency test was 0.9034.

4.2.2 Materials

To research the Japanese students' responses to authentic English material, 15 test items were developed (see Appendix C). Five of these items were based on examples of function-chains taken from an American English textbook, Ginn (1996), where each function-chain dealt with a certain type of question/statement followed by a response. The remaining 10 test items were developed based on the same pattern as shown in Ginn. Then the test's 15 function-chain patterns were classified into five different types, based on categories used in Blundell, Higgens and Middlemiss (1982)[3]. But whereas the categories of function-chains come from Blundell, Higgens and Middlemiss, it was found convenient for the purpose of this study to give clear names to each of the categories. So, as shown below in Table 9, each type of function-chain is followed by an assigned name, which is underlined.

As can be noted below, three test items were prepared for each type of function-chain, with each of the three representing a distinct kind of social relationship — low status to high status, high status to low status, and an equal relationship. This was done in order to assure that each type of function-chain be represented by a variety of social settings.

Table 9. Function-chains in this appropriateness judgment test

---

1. Speaker A: Requesting
   → Speaker B: Offering to do something for someone
   Assistance Function-chain   (Test items ①, ⑥, ⑪)
2. Speaker A: Asking about likes → Speaker B: Expressing likes
   Expressing Liking Function-chain   (Test items ②, ⑦, ⑫)
3. Speaker A: Asking for someone's opinion → Saying you are sure
   Assertion Function-chain   (Test items ③, ⑧, ⑬)
4. Speaker A: Saying you are displeased or angry
   → Speaker B: Calming or reassuring someone
   Reassurance Function-chain   (Test items ④, ⑨, ⑭)
5. Speaker A: Reporting → Speaker B: Saying you are interested
   Expressing Interest Function-chain (Test items ⑤, ⑩, ⑮)
   (15 items in total, i.e., 5 types of function-chains × 3 social relationships.)

4.2.3 Procedure

For each test item the setting, the social relationship of Speakers A and B, and the function-chain type were provided (originally these were written in Japanese for the junior high school students). Also, three possible responses were given for each test item. The students were given instructions in Japanese to rank the responses by order of how appropriately they express the meaning in the function-chain[4]. For example, the question below is an Assertion Function-chain, in which the students had to rank the responses from the most to least appropriate in expressing confident assertion. Similarly, in a Reassurance Function-chain test item they had to rank the responses from the most to least appropriate in giving reassurance, and so on with the other function-chains.

Table 10. An example of the Assertion Function-chain test items

Rank the responses from 1 to 3.
Setting: Classroom. A teacher is introducing a dialogue to kindergarten students using a puppet.
Social relationship: Puppet → Teacher
Function-chain: Asking for someone's opinion → Saying you are sure

A (Puppet): Do you think the children have favorite kinds of days?	kind
B (Teacher): a. I guess so. ( )	種類
b. I'm sure they do. ( )	
c. I think they do. ( )	

It should be noted that while the five test items taken from Ginn (1996) each had originally only one response for each function-chain, two more responses were added for each to allow the students' ranking of responses.

A professor, two associate professors, two adjunct professors, and an assistant language teacher (ALT), all native speakers from the United States, verified that the test items in each function-chain were classified correctly as regarding the type of function-chain involved. They were also in full agreement as to the correct answers. Thus, this study used these six teachers' collective judgment regarding appropriateness as the standard to assess the participants' pragmatic competence.

Also, to reduce the difficulties that could be caused by unfamiliar vocabulary and linguistic structure, translations were given for the words or phrases which the students may not have learned yet.

4.2.4 Scoring

Scores were calculated according to a 2-point system, where 2 points were given when all three responses were correctly ranked, 1 point when the most appropriate response was correctly identified but the other two were in the incorrect order, and no points when the most appropriate response was not correctly identified. As mentioned, each function-chain included three test items, therefore the maximum score for each function-chain was 6 points (2 points multiplied by 3 test items).

4.2.5 Means of analysis

In order to analyze the obtained data, a one-way layout MANOVA was conducted, where the independent variable was level of proficiency in English (between-subjects, 2 levels: a relatively high proficiency group and a low proficiency group). The dependent variables were the sum of the scores for each type of function-chain (5 types: Assistance, Liking, Assertion, Reassurance, Interest). All the analyses were performed with SPSS ver.11.

4.3 Results

The descriptive statistics[5] and the results of the one-way layout MANOVA are presented in Tables 11, 12, and 13.

In Table 11, sample size (N), means, and standard deviations (SD) are displayed.

It can be seen from Tables 11 and 12, that there was a significant difference between the levels of proficiency in English, with the relatively high proficiency group's score being higher than the low proficiency group's (Wilks' lambda: $F(5,144) = 4.146, p < .01$).

Table 11. Descriptive statistics

	Test of Practical English	N	Mean	SD
Assistance (Total)	Low	74	2.270	1.358
	High	76	2.329	1.182
	Total	150	2.300	1.268
Liking (Total)	Low	74	4.811	1.421
	High	76	5.211	.998
	Total	150	5.011	1.237
Assertion (Total)	Low	74	2.568	1.605
	High	76	3.539	1.390
	Total	150	3.054	1.573
Reassurance (Total)	Low	74	2.176	1.115
	High	76	2.553	1.310
	Total	150	2.364	1.228
Interest (Total)	Low	74	1.986	1.104
	High	76	2.250	.954
	Total	150	2.118	1.036

Table 12. Multivariate tests[b]

Effect		Value	Hypothesis F	df	Error df	Sig.
Intercept	Pillai's trace	.961	703.086[a]	5.000	144.000	.000
	Wilks' lambda	.039	703.086[a]	5.000	144.000	.000
	Hotelling's trace	24.413	703.086[a]	5.000	144.000	.000
	Roy's largest root	24.413	703.086[a]	5.000	144.000	.000
Level of proficiency in English	Pillai's trace	.126	4.146[a]	5.000	144.000	.002
	Wilks' lambda	.874	4.146[a]	5.000	144.000	.002
	Hotelling's trace	.144	4.146[a]	5.000	144.000	.002
	Roy's largest root	.144	4.146[a]	5.000	144.000	.002

a. Exact statistic
b. Design: Intercept + Level of proficiency in English

In addition to the multivariate tests, simple univariate F tests on each of the dependent variables were also performed (see Table 13).

Table 13. Tests of between-subjects effects

Source	Dependent Variable		Type III Sum of Squares	df	Mean Square	F	Sig.
Corrected Model	Assistance	(Total)	.129[a]	1	.129	.080	.778
	Liking	(Total)	5.990[b]	1	5.990	3.994	.047
	Assertion	(Total)	35.416[c]	1	35.416	15.738	.000
	Reassurance	(Total)	5.328[d]	1	5.328	3.592	.060
	Interest	(Total)	2.604[e]	1	2.604	2.451	.120
Intercept	Assistance	(Total)	793.089	1	793.089	490.357	.000
	Liking	(Total)	3765.350	1	3765.350	2510.427	.000
	Assertion	(Total)	1398.350	1	1398.350	621.407	.000
	Reassurance	(Total)	838.234	1	838.234	565.173	.000
	Interest	(Total)	672.924	1	672.924	633.394	.000
Level of Proficiency in English	Assistance	(Total)	.129	1	.129	.080	.778
	Liking	(Total)	5.990	1	5.990	3.994	.047
	Assertion	(Total)	35.416	1	35.416	15.738	.000
	Reassurance	(Total)	5.328	1	5.328	3.592	.060
	Interest	(Total)	2.604	1	2.604	2.451	.120
Error	Assistance	(Total)	239.371	148	1.617		
	Liking	(Total)	221.983	148	1.500		
	Assertion	(Total)	333.044	148	2.250		
	Reassurance	(Total)	219.506	148	1.483		
	Interest	(Total)	157.236	148	1.062		
Total	Assistance	(Total)	1033.000	150			
	Liking	(Total)	3998.000	150			
	Assertion	(Total)	1773.000	150			
	Reassurance	(Total)	1065.000	150			
	Interest	(Total)	834.000	150			
Corrected Total	Assistance	(Total)	239.500	149			
	Liking	(Total)	227.973	149			
	Assertion	(Total)	368.460	149			
	Reassurance	(Total)	224.833	149			
	Interest	(Total)	159.840	149			

a. $R^2 = .001$ (adjusted $R^2 = -.006$)
b. $R^2 = .026$ (adjusted $R^2 = .020$)
c. $R^2 = .096$ (adjusted $R^2 = .090$)
d. $R^2 = .024$ (adjusted $R^2 = .017$)
e. $R^2 = .016$ (adjusted $R^2 = .010$)

As for the type of function-chains, as is clear from Table 13, for the Expressing Liking Function-chain and the Assertion Function-chain, there was a significant difference between the levels of proficiency in English, with the relatively high proficiency group's score being higher than the low proficiency group's (Liking: $F\,(1,148) = 3.994$, $p < .05$; Assertion: $F\,(1,148) = 15.738$, $p < .001$)).

4.4 Discussion

In this study, two types of function-chains (the Expressing Liking Function-chain and the Assertion Function-chain) were found to show a significant difference in appropriateness judgment scores between the levels of proficiency in English, with the relatively high proficiency group's score being higher than the low proficiency group's. It suggests that as students gain English proficiency they find it increasingly easy to identify appropriateness in these types of function-chains. On the other hand, even the relatively high proficiency group had difficulty recognizing appropriateness for the other three types of function-chains. That is, we can say that for these types of function-chains the junior high school students' English proficiency level did not guarantee pragmatic competence. This result could help shed light on early developmental patterns in interlanguage pragmatic knowledge. Study 3 is the subject of the next chapter, which extends the range of participants and investigates more closely the route of development as regards recognition of appropriateness.

Notes

[1] Test of Practical English: the Test of Practical English was prepared by The Society for Testing English Proficiency, Inc., and authorized by the Japanese Ministry of Education, Culture, Sports, Science and Technology in the years 2000-2002.

[2] median: the value of the middle item or score when the scores in a sample are arranged in order from lowest to highest. The median is therefore the score that divides the sample into two equal parts. It is the most appropriate measure of the central tendency for data arranged in an "ordinal scale" or a "rank scale." (Richards and Schmidt, 2002)

[3] As for Reporting, which is not included in Blundell, Higgens, and Middlemiss, the author referred to van Ek (1976).

[4] In this experiment, appropriateness encompasses the linguistic realizations which express the emotive force of the function in question. Among the other studies dealing with emotive force, we can see Rintell (1984). According to Kasper and Dahl (1991), Rintell (1984) examined how non-native speakers perceive expressions of emotion. After listening to taped dialogues, participants were asked to identify the expressed emotion on an answer sheet and rate its intensity on a scale. No effects were found for age or sex on the intensity scores. The two variables that did determine non-native speakers' perception of emotive force were L1 and proficiency. Chinese subjects' responses differed consistently from those of Arabic and Spanish students, and beginners' perceptions contrasted sharply with those of the intermediate and advanced groups.

[5] descriptive statistics: statistical procedures that are used to describe, organize and summarize the important general characteristics of a set of data. A descriptive statistic is a number that represents some feature of the data, such as measures of central tendency and dispersions. (Richards and Schmidt, 2002)

Chapter 5
Study 3 (Analysis 1): The recognition of the appropriateness of actual utterances by junior high students, university students, and native speakers of English

5.1 Objectives

In the previous chapter, the author focused on beginning English learners (Japanese junior high school students) and investigated the relation between proficiency and pragmatic development. Two types of function-chains were found to show a significant difference in appropriateness judgment scores between the levels of proficiency in English.

The present study extends the range of participants and investigates more closely the effect of the level of proficiency in English and the type of function-chains on the recognition of appropriateness. The following research questions are the foci of this study.

(1) Do the study groups, representing different levels of English proficiency, show a statistically significant difference in their recognition of the appropriateness of the function-chain?

(2) Does the amount of improvement, as regards recognition of appropriateness between levels of English proficiency, vary considerably depending on the type of function-chain involved?

(3) Do the different types of function-chains present distinctly different levels of difficulty for the test participants?

5.2 Method

5.2.1 Participants

The participants in this study were 94 Japanese second year junior high school students (J), 86 Japanese third year university students, and 41 university students who were native speakers from the United States (NS)[1]. The Japanese university students were further sub-divided into a group of 35 English major students with experience of study abroad (U$^+$), and a group of 51 students who had majors other than English and lacked experience of study abroad (U$^-$). The U$^+$ students scored, on an average, 539 on the TOEFL. They had all spent at least four months studying English intensively and attending regular courses at universities abroad, during which time they stayed with homestay families. On the other hand, the U$^-$ students did not have such experience. Thus, there was a total of four groups included in the study, all with varying levels of proficiency and experience in English[2].

5.2.2 Materials

The same five types of function-chains as in Study 2 (i.e., Assistance, Liking, Assertion, Reassurance, Interest) were included in the test. The test items then presented three distinct kinds of social relationships for each type of function-chain: low status to high status, high status to low status, and an equal relationship. Each type of social relationship was then represented by two distinct settings. Each setting in turn presented two possible responses (a. and b.) to each statement, one appropriate and one inappropriate. Which of the responses (a. and b.) was appropriate or inappropriate was decided at random. As the testees had to make a separate judgment for each response as to its appropriateness or inappropriateness, each response was considered to be a separate test item. Thus, 60 test items in all (5 types of function-chains × 3 social relationships × 2 settings × 2 responses [appropriate/inappropriate]) were prepared for this study (see Appendix D^3).

5.2.3 Procedure

The results obtained in the previous chapter were based on written material where prosodic features[4] were not considered. However, it seems possible that these factors may have an effect on the perception of appropriateness of the function-chains. Therefore, in this study the appropriateness judgment test was presented in two mediums — 1) a questionnaire in written form and 2) a CD recording in audio form. The participants read and listened, paying attention to 1) the social relationships (a teacher talking to a student, a student talking to a teacher, or a student talking to a student) and 2) the settings. The participants rated each response on a scale of appropriateness, ranging from 1 (inappropriate) to 3 (appropriate) (see Table 14).

Table 14. An example of the Assistance Function-chain test items

Please rate each response on the scale of appropriateness, with (1) being inappropriate, and (3) being appropriate. Setting: In a classroom. The teacher requests help in moving a table. A (Teacher)   Will you help me? B (Student)   a. Of course.   1 : 2 : 3   b. Yes, if I have to.   1 : 2 : 3

Five Americans, all residing and teaching English in Japan, verified that the test items in each function-chain were classified correctly as regarding the type of function-chain involved. They were also in full agreement as to the rating of appropriateness. That is, all of them judged one of the responses to be appropriate (i.e., rated as 3) and the other to be inappropriate (i.e., rated as 1). Thus, this study used these five teachers' collective judgment regarding appropriateness as the standard to assess the participants' pragmatic competence[5].

To reduce the difficulties that could be caused by unfamiliar vocabulary and linguistic structure, translations were given for words or phrases which the junior high school students may not have learned yet. Also, the instructions, the setting, and the social relationship of Speakers A and B were written in Japanese for the Japanese students (see Appendix E).

5.2.4 Scoring

Scores were calculated according to a 3-point system, where 3 points were given when the responses were correctly rated, 2 points when they judged the response to be "neither" (i.e., when they selected 2 as the rating), and 1 point when they judged the appropriate response to be inappropriate, and the inappropriate response to be appropriate. As mentioned, each function-chain included 12 test items (3 social relationships × 2 settings × 2 responses [appropriate/inappropriate]). Therefore, the maximum score for each function-chain was 36 points (3 points multiplied by 12 test items). In the analysis of these results, the z-score[6] was used to compare the relative difficulty that the different types of function-chains presented for the groups involved. Each student's z-score for each type of function-chain was computed using the mean and the standard deviation (*SD*) of all the participants.

5.2.5 Means of analysis

In order to analyze the obtained data, a two-way layout ANOVA was conducted, where the independent variables were (1) level of proficiency in English (between-subjects, 4 levels: J, U⁻, U⁺, NS) and (2) function-chains (within-subject, 5 levels: Assistance, Liking, Assertion, Reassurance, Interest). The dependent variable was the sum of the scores for each type of function-chain. All the analyses were performed with ANOVA 4 (ver.1.11 β).

5.3 Results

The mean and the standard deviation (*SD*) of the z-score for each type of function-chain are presented in Table 15.

Table 15. Descriptive statistics

		N	*Mean*	*SD*
Assistance	J	94	− 0.584	1.006
	U⁻	51	0.129	0.823
	U⁺	35	0.529	0.679
	NS	41	0.726	0.493
Liking	J	94	− 0.337	1.082
	U⁻	51	− 0.015	0.889
	U⁺	35	0.357	0.690
	NS	41	0.486	0.830
Assertion	J	94	− 0.443	1.054
	U⁻	51	0.093	0.816
	U⁺	35	0.301	0.835
	NS	41	0.643	0.667
Reassurance	J	94	− 0.422	1.118
	U⁻	51	0.127	0.778
	U⁺	35	0.737	0.412
	NS	41	0.181	0.822
Interest	J	94	− 0.473	0.819
	U⁻	51	− 0.180	0.865
	U⁺	35	0.429	0.702
	NS	41	0.941	0.940

The results of this analysis can be grouped into the following two areas: 1) the main effect of each independent variable and the interaction of the two independent variables; and 2) the simple main effect of the interaction between proficiency level and function-chain.

First, we shall examine the main effect that each independent variable has, as well as the interaction between the two independent variables.

As Table 16 indicates, (1) the difference between the levels of proficiency in English was statistically significant (F (3, 217) = 28.857, $p < .001$). (2) The interaction between the level of proficiency in English and the type of function-chain was significant (F (12,868) = 3.976, $p < .001$).

Table 16. Table of ANOVA

source	SS	df	MS	F	p
(1) A: Level of proficiency in English	162.737	3	54.246	28.857	0.000[****]
error [S(A)]	407.925	217	1.880		
B: Function-chain	0.670	4	0.168	0.316	0.868
(2) AB	25.325	12	2.110	3.976	0.000[****]
error [BS(A)]	460.709	868	0.531		

[****]$p < .001$

Thus, the interaction between the level of proficiency in English and the type of function-chain was significant. Therefore, the next step was the examination of the simple main effect of the interaction between proficiency level and function-chain, the results of which are presented in Table 17 (see next page).

As is clear from Table 17, (1) for all of the five types of function-chains, the difference between the levels of proficiency was statistically significant — Assistance: F (3,1085) = 20.097, $p < .001$; Liking: F (3,1085) = 8.350, $p < .001$; Assertion: F (3, 1085) = 12.442, $p < .001$; Reassurance; F (3,1085) = 13.474, $p < .001$; Interest: F (3,1085) =

23.940, $p < .001$. (2) There was a significant difference between the function-chains for those students with experience of study abroad (U^+) ($F(4,868) = 2.658, p < .05$). (3) There was also a significant difference between the function-chains for the group of native speakers (NS) ($F(4,868) = 7.291, p < .001$).

Table 17. Simple main effect of interaction between proficiency level and function-chain

	effect		SS	df	MS	F	p
(1)	Proficiency level	(Assistance)	48.267	3	16.089	20.097	0.000****
(1)	Proficiency level	(Liking)	20.055	3	6.685	8.350	0.000****
(1)	Proficiency level	(Assertion)	29.882	3	9.961	12.442	0.000****
(1)	Proficiency level	(Reassurance)	32.361	3	10.787	13.474	0.000****
(1)	Proficiency level	(Interest)	57.497	3	19.166	23.940	0.000****
	error			1085	0.801		
	Function-chain	(J)	1.539	4	0.385	0.725	0.575
	Function-chain	(U^-)	3.334	4	0.834	1.570	0.180
(2)	Function-chain	(U^+)	5.642	4	1.411	2.658	0.032*
(3)	Function-chain	(NS)	15.479	4	3.870	7.291	0.000****
	error			868	0.531		

$^*p < .05, ^{**}p < .01, ^{***}p < .005, ^{****}p < .001$

Next, multiple comparisons were conducted as follows: 1) the comparison between the levels of proficiency in English for each type of function-chain, 2) the comparison between the function-chains for the U^+ group, and 3) the comparison between the function-chains for the NS group. A post hoc analysis (Ryan's method) was computed to study the differences between the means (the significance level was $p = .05$).

We shall now look carefully into the results of the comparison between the levels of proficiency in English for each type of function-chain. Firstly, for the Assistance Function-chain, multiple comparisons of the levels of proficiency yielded the following. The mean of the z-scores for the four groups of participants — J, U^-, U^+, and NS — in the Assistance Function-chain were $-0.584, 0.129, 0.529$, and 0.726 respectively. As a result of multiple comparisons, significant differences were found between the following pairs at the .05 level: pairs NS — J, NS — U^-, U^+— J, and U^-— J. However, there was no significant difference between the pairs NS — U^+, and U^+— U^- at the .05 level (see Table 18).

Table 18. Multiple comparisons of the levels of proficiency for the Assistance Function-chain

	J	U^-	U^+	NS
Mean :	− 0.584	0.129	0.529	0.726
N :	94	51	35	41

pair	r	nominal level	t	p	sig.
NS — J	4	0.008	7.822	0.000	s.
NS — U^-	3	0.013	3.178	0.002	s.
U^+— J	3	0.013	6.279	0.000	s.
NS — U^+	2	0.025	0.959	0.338	n.s.
U^+—U^-	2	0.025	2.032	0.042	n.s.
U^-— J	2	0.025	4.584	0.000	s.

$MSe = 0.801$, $df = 1085$, significance level $= 0.050$

Thus, the participants' scores on the Assistance Function-chain were shown to be as follows ($MSe = 0.800585$, $p < .05$):

$$J < U^- < NS$$
$$J < U^+ \fallingdotseq NS$$
$$U^- \fallingdotseq U^+$$

As for the appropriateness judgment scores for the Assistance Function-chain, the university students and the native speakers were higher than the junior high school students. Also, the native speakers were higher than the U^- students.

In the case of the Expressing Liking Function-chain, multiple comparisons of the levels of proficiency showed the following results. The mean of the z-scores for the four groups of participants — J, U^-, U^+, and NS — in the Expressing Liking Function-chain were − 0.337, − 0.015, 0.357, and 0.486 respectively. As a result of multiple comparisons, significant differences were found between the following pairs at the .05 level: pairs NS — J, NS — U^-, and U^+ — J. However, there was no significant difference between the pairs NS — U^+, U^+ — U^-, and U^- — J at the .05 level (see Table 19).

Table 19. Multiple comparisons of the levels of proficiency for the Expressing Liking Function-chain

	J	U^-	U^+	NS		
Mean:	− 0.337	−0.015	0.357	0.486		
N :	94	51	35	41		
pair	r	nominal level	t	p	sig.
NS — J	4	0.008	4.914	0.000	s.
NS — U^-	3	0.013	2.667	0.008	s.
U^+ — J	3	0.013	3.919	0.000	s.
NS — U^+	2	0.025	0.624	0.533	n.s.
U^+ — U^-	2	0.025	1.894	0.058	n.s.
U^- — J	2	0.025	2.071	0.039	n.s.

$MSe = 0.801$, $df = 1085$, significance level $= 0.050$

Thus, the participants' scores on the Expressing Liking Function-chain were as follows ($MSe = 0.800585, p < .05$):

$$J < U^+ \fallingdotseq NS$$
$$U^- < NS$$
$$J \fallingdotseq U^-$$
$$U^- \fallingdotseq U^+$$

As for the appropriateness judgment scores for the Expressing Liking Function-chain, the U^+ students and the native speakers scored higher than the junior high school students. Also, the native speakers were higher than the U^- students.

For the Assertion Function-chain, multiple comparisons of the levels of proficiency showed the following results. The mean of the z-scores for the four groups of participants — J, U^-, U^+, and NS — in the Assertion Function-chain were -0.443, 0.093, 0.301, and 0.643 respectively. As a result of multiple comparisons, significant differences were found between the following pairs at the .05 level: pairs NS — J, NS — U^-, U^+— J, and U^-— J. However, there was no significant difference between the pairs NS — U^+ and U^+— U^- at the .05 level (see Table 20).

Table 20. Multiple comparisons of the levels of proficiency for the Assertion Function-chain

	J	U^-	U^+	NS
Mean:	−0.443	0.093	0.301	0.643
N :	94	51	35	41

pair	r	nominal level	t	p	sig.
NS — J	4	0.008	6.489	0.000	s.
NS — U^-	3	0.013	2.935	0.003	s.
U^+— J	3	0.013	4.202	0.000	s.
NS — U^+	2	0.025	1.662	0.097	n.s.
U^+—U^-	2	0.025	1.062	0.288	n.s.
U^-— J	2	0.025	3.444	0.001	s.

$MSe = 0.801$, $df = 1085$, significance level $= 0.050$

Thus, the participants' scores on the Assertion Function-chain were shown to be as follows ($MSe = 0.800585$, $p < .05$):

$$J < U^- < NS$$
$$J < U^+ \fallingdotseq NS$$
$$U^- \fallingdotseq U^+$$

As for the appropriateness judgment scores for the Assertion Function-chain, the university students and the native speakers were higher than the junior high school students. Also, the native speakers were higher than the U^- students.

As regards the Reassurance Function-chain, multiple comparisons of the levels of proficiency brought to light the following. The mean of the z-scores for the four groups of participants — J, U^-, U^+, and NS — in the Reassurance Function-chain were -0.422, 0.127, 0.737, and 0.181 respectively. As a result of multiple comparisons, significant differences were found between the following pairs at the .05 level: pairs U^+—J, U^+—U^-, NS — J, U^+— NS, and U^-— J. However, there was no significant difference between NS and U^- at the .05 level (see Table 21).

Table 21. Multiple comparisons of the levels of proficiency for the Reassurance Function-chain

	J	U^-	U^+	NS
Mean:	−0.422	0.127	0.737	0.181
N:	94	51	35	41

pair	r	nominal level	t	p	sig.
U^+— J	4	0.008	6.542	0.000	s.
U^+—U^-	3	0.013	3.103	0.002	s.
NS — J	3	0.013	3.604	0.000	s.
U^+— NS	2	0.025	2.698	0.007	s.
NS — U^-	2	0.025	0.287	0.774	n.s.
U^-— J	2	0.025	3.533	0.000	s.

$MSe = 0.801$, $df = 1085$, significance level $= 0.050$

Thus, the participants' scores on the Reassurance Function-chain were shown to be as follows ($MSe = 0.800585$, $p < .05$):

$$J < U^- \fallingdotseq NS < U^+$$

As for the appropriateness judgment scores for the Reassurance Function-chain, the university students and the native speakers were higher than the junior high school students. Also, the U^+ students were higher than the U^- students. Here, we see that the appropriateness judgment score of the Japanese U^+ students was higher than that of the native speakers. In order to explain this result, in-depth qualitative analysis will be required.

Finally, in the case of the Expressing Interest Function-chain, multiple comparisons of the levels of proficiency showed the following results. The mean of the z-scores for the four groups of participants — J, U^-, U^+, and NS — in the Expressing Interest Function-chain were -0.473, -0.180, 0.429, 0.941 respectively. As a result of multiple comparisons, significant differences were found between the following pairs at the .05 level: pairs NS — J, NS — U^-, U^+— J, NS — U^+, and U^+— U^-. However, there was no significant difference between U^- and J at the .05 level (see Table 22).

Table 22. **Multiple comparisons of the levels of proficiency for the Expressing Interest Function-chain**

	J	U^-	U^+	NS
Mean:	−0.473	−0.180	0.429	0.941
N:	94	51	35	41

pair	r	nominal level	t	p	sig.
NS — J	4	0.008	8.439	0.000	s.
NS — U^-	3	0.013	5.971	0.000	s.
U^+— J	3	0.013	5.090	0.000	s.
NS — U^+	2	0.025	2.483	0.013	s.
U^+—U^-	2	0.025	3.102	0.002	s.
U^-— J	2	0.025	1.880	0.060	n.s.

$MSe = 0.801$, $df = 1085$, significance level $= 0.050$

Thus, the participants' scores on the Expressing Interest Function-chain were shown to be as follows ($MSe = 0.800585, p < .05$):

$$J \fallingdotseq U^- < U^+ < NS$$

As for the appropriateness judgment scores for the Expressing Interest Function-chain, the U^+ students and the native speakers scored higher than the junior high school students and the U^- students.

So far, we have looked into the results of the comparison between the levels of proficiency in English for each type of function-chain. Next, as was mentioned above, multiple comparisons between the function-chains for the U^+ and NS groups were also computed.

For the U^+ group, multiple comparisons of the function-chains showed the following results. The mean of the z-scores for the five types of function-chains — Assistance, Liking, Assertion, Reassurance, and Interest — in the U^+ group were 0.529, 0.357, 0.301, 0.737, and 0.429 respectively. In Table 17, the simple main effect of interaction between proficiency level and function-chain showed that there was a significant difference between the function-chains for the U^+ students ($F(4,868) = 2.658, p < .05$). However, the results of the post hoc analysis (Ryan's method) showed that there was no significant difference between any pairs of the function-chains at the .05 level (see Table 23).

As regards the results of the NS group, multiple comparisons of the function-chains yielded the following. The mean of the z-scores for the five types of function-chains — Assistance, Liking, Assertion, Reassurance, and Interest — in the NS group were 0.726, 0.486, 0.643, 0.181, and 0.941 respectively. As a result of multiple comparisons, significant differences were found between the following pairs at the .05 level: pairs Interest — Reassurance, Interest — Liking, Assistance — Reassurance,

Table 23. Multiple comparisons of the function-chains for the U⁺ group

	Assistance	Liking	Assertion	Reassurance	Interest
Mean:	0.529	0.357	0.301	0.737	0.429
N:	35	35	35	35	35

pair	r	nominal level	t	p	sig.
Reassurance — Assertion	5	0.005	2.501	0.013	n.s.
Reassurance — Liking	4	0.007	2.178	0.030	n.s.
Assistance — Assertion	4	0.007	1.305	0.192	n.s.
Reassurance — Interest	3	0.010	1.765	0.078	n.s.
Assistance — Liking	3	0.010	0.982	0.326	n.s.
Interest — Assertion	3	0.010	0.736	0.462	n.s.
Assistance — Interest	2	0.020	0.569	0.569	n.s.
Reassurance — Assistance	2	0.020	1.196	0.232	n.s.
Interest — Liking	2	0.020	0.413	0.680	n.s.
Liking — Assertion	2	0.020	0.323	0.747	n.s.

$MSe = 0.531$, $df = 868$, significance level $= 0.050$

and Assertion — Reassurance. However, there was no significant difference between the pairs Interest — Assertion, Assistance — Liking, Assistance — Assertion, Interest — Assistance, Assertion — Liking, and Liking — Reassurance at the .05 level (see Table 24).

Table 24. Multiple comparisons of the function-chains for the NS group

	Assistance	Liking	Assertion	Reassurance	Interest
Mean:	0.726	0.486	0.643	0.181	0.941
N:	41	41	41	41	41

pair	r	nominal level	t	p	sig.
Interest — Reassurance	5	0.005	4.719	0.000	s.
Interest — Liking	4	0.007	2.826	0.005	s.
Assistance — Reassurance	4	0.007	3.385	0.001	s.
Interest — Assertion	3	0.010	1.847	0.065	n.s.
Assistance — Liking	3	0.010	1.491	0.136	n.s.
Assertion — Reassurance	3	0.010	2.873	0.004	s.
Assistance — Assertion	2	0.020	0.512	0.609	n.s.
Interest — Assistance	2	0.020	1.334	0.182	n.s.
Assertion — Liking	2	0.020	0.979	0.328	n.s.
Liking — Reassurance	2	0.020	1.894	0.059	n.s.

$MSe = 0.531$, $df = 868$, significance level $= 0.050$

Thus, the native speakers' scores on the five types of function-chains were shown to be as follows ($MSe = 0.530771, p < .05$):

> Reassurance $<$ Assertion $\fallingdotseq$ Assistance $\fallingdotseq$ Interest
> Liking $<$ Interest

5.4 Discussion

The results of this study show the following.

First, the four study groups, representing different levels of English proficiency, did show a statistically significant difference in their recognition of the appropriateness of the five types of function-chains used in the test.

However, depending on the type of function-chain involved, the amount of improvement, as regards recognition of appropriateness between levels of English proficiency, varied considerably. As for the appropriateness judgment scores for the Assistance, Assertion, and Reassurance Function-chains, the university students and the native speakers were higher than the junior high school students. In the case of the Expressing Liking and Interest Function-chains, there was no significant difference between the junior high school students and the university students without experience of study abroad. That is to say, each function-chain shows its own unique rate and route of development for the study groups involved. Here, it is noteworthy that for the Reassurance Function-chain, the appropriateness judgment score of the Japanese U$^+$ students was higher than that of the native speakers. One explanation for this result may be that the Japanese U$^+$ students were over-sensitive (overly strict) in their judgment as to what constitutes appropriate language when compared to native speakers. Carrell and Konneker (1981) report a similar phenomenon that non-native speakers are more sensitive (or over-sensitive) to politeness values than native speakers[7]. In the case of the present study, a correct interpretation of the results will require further investigation.

As for the relative level of difficulty of the types of function-chains, an interesting observation can be made when comparing Japanese students with native speakers. Namely, the different types of function-chains presented an almost equal level of difficulty for the Japanese students. For native speakers, however, some types of function-chains presented distinctly different levels of difficulty. This differentiation of the relative level of difficulty seems to suggest a direction of language acquisition.

This study has provided some fundamental information about the process by which learners of English develop pragmatic competence as regards function-chains. However, the following characteristics of Japanese students remain to be identified: the areas of difficulty specific to each group, those areas difficult for Japanese EFL learners irrespective of English proficiency level, and the areas in which Japanese EFL learners were over-sensitive (overly strict) in their judgment as to what constituted appropriate language. In order to investigate these areas, we should take further steps. That is, we should conduct a quantitative analysis again based on the participants' score on each test item, and then employ a qualitative analysis along with the quantitative results in order to recognize any useful and informative patterns that might emerge. The next chapter summarizes the results of the analysis using both quantitative and qualitative research methods.

Notes

[1] As for the native speakers from the United States, the researcher's application to use students as testees was reviewed and approved by the Institutional Review Board (IRB) of California State University, San Bernardino.

[2] It is not feasible to give the same English proficiency test to both junior high school students (beginning English learners) and university students. Therefore, no proficiency tests were administered, but it was assumed that the four different levels of experience with English also represented distinct proficiency levels. In Trosborg (1995), we can see a similar case. Trosborg examined the requests, complaints, and apologies of three groups of Danish learners of English: secondary school grade 9, high school and commercial school, and university students. In that study as well, proficiency tests were not administered, as it was assumed that the three educational levels also represented proficiency levels.

[3] The informed consent and debriefing statements in Appendix D include an e-mail address (tozasa@hiroshima-u.ac.jp), which is no longer valid. It pertained to Dr. Ozasa, formerly with Hiroshima University, but now a professor at Fukuyama Heisei University.

[4] prosodic features: sound characteristics which affect whole sequences of syllables. They may involve, for instance, the relative loudness or duration of syllables, changes in the pitch of a speaker's voice and the choice of pitch level. (Richards and Schmidt, 2002)

[5] The reason why a group of teachers' judgment was used, rather than the judgment of the 41 native speakers who took the test, was the following. Even among native speakers there may be those who are relatively liberal in their speech standards, and thus likely to tolerate non-standard usage. However, it was considered that a group of teachers, as compared with students, would tend to be more strict in their standard of usage.

[6] z-score: (in statistics) a standard score expressed in standard deviation units with a mean of zero and a standard deviation of one. As the following formula for a z-score shows:

$$z = \frac{X - \overline{X}}{SD}$$

where X = the raw score
$\bar{X}$ = the mean
SD = the standard deviation,
a raw score is expressed in terms of the number of standard deviations by which it deviates from the mean. Thus, a student with a z-score of -1.0 is one standard deviation below the mean. (Richards and Schmidt, 2002). In the present study, the z-score of each student was calculated from the X and the SD of all the participants.

[7] Carrell and Konneker (1981) looked at non-native speakers' perception of politeness for eight different request strategies. Participants were presented with cards specifying different request contexts and the eight strategies, and then asked to sort the strategies according to level of politeness. The order of perceived politeness obtained for each strategy suggested that non-native speakers both overdifferentiate request strategies (they perceived seven politeness levels, whereas the native speakers distinguished only five), and in some cases underdifferentiate strategies (they did not recognize some of the same boundaries between strategies that native speakers did) (Kasper and Dahl, 1991). Carrell and Konneker state that it is noteworthy that non-native speakers show over-sensitivity to politeness values, but they only report the phenomenon and do not study the causes. Non-native speakers' over-sensitivity is certainly an interesting phenomenon, whose nature and causes would be a worthwhile subject for a more in-depth study (Ozasa (Ed.), 1983).

Chapter 6
Study 3 (Analysis 2): The acquisition of English function-chains viewed qualitatively

6.1 Objectives

In the previous chapter, the range of participants was extended and the relationship between the level of proficiency in English and the type of function-chain was investigated. Also, the rate and route of development as regards recognition of appropriateness for the five types of function-chains was clarified.

The present study examines each group's judgment of appropriateness for each test item (each dialogue) in more detail, and tries to identify any informative patterns in their judgment that might emerge. The following research questions are the foci of this study.

(1) What kinds of dialogues, if any, are difficult specifically for each proficiency level group?
(2) What kinds of dialogues, if any, are difficult for Japanese EFL learners irrespective of English proficiency level?
(3) To what kinds of dialogues, if any, were Japanese EFL learners oversensitive in their judgment as to what constituted appropriate language?

6.2 Method

6.2.1 Participants, materials, procedure, and scoring

As regards the participants, materials, procedure, and scoring, these were the same as those mentioned in the previous chapter (Analysis 1).

6.2.2 Means of analysis

First, a quantitative analysis was again conducted. This time, in order to closely examine each group's appropriateness judgment for each test item, a one-way layout ANOVA was conducted based on the score for each test item. The independent variable was the level of proficiency in English (between-subjects, 4 levels: J, U $^-$, U $^+$, NS). The dependent variable was the participants' scores on the appropriateness judgment test. This analysis did not compare the relative difficulty that each test item presented for the groups involved; therefore, the z-score was not used this time. All the analyses were performed with SPSS ver.11.

Then, qualitative analysis[1] was employed, along with the quantitative results from the one-way layout ANOVA, which proved to be useful and complementary for the purposes of this study. Matrices were used as a means of displaying, analyzing, and synthesizing the data in order to recognize any useful and informative patterns that might emerge[2].

6.3 Results

The descriptive statistics are presented in Table 25 (see pages 66, 67, and 68). Following that, the result of the one-way layout ANOVA is displayed in Table 26 (see pages 68, 69, and 70).

Table 25. Descriptive statistics

Assistance Function-chain (results for test items)

		N	Mean	SD			N	Mean	SD
13a	J	94	2.64	.637	22a	J	94	2.51	.800
	U −	51	2.78	.541		U −	51	2.78	.577
	U +	35	2.69	.631		U +	35	2.83	.568
	NS	41	3.00	.000		NS	41	2.98	.156
	Total	221	2.75	.563		Total	221	2.71	.659
13b	J	94	2.38	.764	22b	J	94	2.61	.722
	U −	51	2.22	.832		U −	51	2.69	.707
	U +	35	2.31	.867		U +	35	2.74	.657
	NS	41	2.93	.264		NS	41	2.98	.156
	Total	221	2.43	.770		Total	221	2.71	.650
14a	J	94	2.82	.507	23a	J	94	2.24	.758
	U −	51	2.92	.272		U −	51	2.39	.723
	U +	35	2.94	.236		U +	35	2.74	.505
	NS	41	2.29	.750		NS	41	2.95	.218
	Total	221	2.76	.538		Total	221	2.49	.698
14b	J	94	2.88	.355	23b	J	94	2.71	.561
	U −	51	3.00	.000		U −	51	2.90	.361
	U +	35	3.00	.000		U +	35	2.97	.169
	NS	41	2.93	.264		NS	41	2.93	.346
	Total	221	2.94	.262		Total	221	2.84	.448
15a	J	94	1.95	.920	24a	J	94	2.51	.715
	U −	51	2.59	.779		U −	51	2.67	.653
	U +	35	2.80	.531		U +	35	2.89	.404
	NS	41	2.95	.218		NS	41	2.63	.662
	Total	221	2.42	.852		Total	221	2.63	.659
15b	J	94	1.93	.942	24b	J	94	2.69	.605
	U −	51	2.51	.834		U −	51	2.92	.392
	U +	35	2.89	.471		U +	35	2.97	.169
	NS	41	2.93	.264		NS	41	2.98	.156
	Total	221	2.40	.876		Total	221	2.84	.464
					Assistance (Total)	J	94	29.87	3.545
						U −	51	32.37	2.912
						U +	35	33.77	2.414
						NS	41	34.46	1.748
						Total	221	31.92	3.505

Expressing Liking Function-chain (results for test items)

		N	Mean	SD			N	Mean	SD
10a	J	94	2.48	.786	19a	J	94	2.34	.712
	U −	51	2.71	.642		U −	51	2.55	.642
	U +	35	2.94	.236		U +	35	2.60	.651
	NS	41	2.90	.374		NS	41	2.22	.852
	Total	221	2.68	.653		Total	221	2.41	.724
10b	J	94	2.65	.683	19b	J	94	2.82	.507
	U −	51	2.76	.551		U −	51	3.00	.000
	U +	35	2.94	.338		U +	35	2.97	.169
	NS	41	2.85	.422		NS	41	2.95	.218
	Total	221	2.76	.573		Total	221	2.91	.358
11a	J	94	1.93	.883	20a	J	94	2.03	.933
	U −	51	1.84	.809		U −	51	2.10	.944
	U +	35	1.94	.725		U +	35	2.46	.741
	NS	41	1.90	.800		NS	41	2.49	.746
	Total	221	1.90	.823		Total	221	2.20	.892
11b	J	94	2.32	.779	20b	J	94	2.32	.832
	U −	51	2.78	.503		U −	51	2.41	.779
	U +	35	2.91	.373		U +	35	2.74	.561
	NS	41	2.93	.346		NS	41	3.00	.000
	Total	221	2.63	.658		Total	221	2.53	.742
12a	J	94	2.83	.478	21a	J	94	2.09	.912
	U −	51	2.82	.555		U −	51	2.14	.849
	U +	35	2.83	.514		U +	35	2.11	.867
	NS	41	2.88	.458		NS	41	2.63	.662
	Total	221	2.84	.496		Total	221	2.20	.868
12b	J	94	2.45	.728	21b	J	94	2.29	.771
	U −	51	2.04	.824		U −	51	2.67	.653
	U +	35	2.26	.701		U +	35	2.60	.651
	NS	41	2.07	.818		NS	41	3.00	.000
	Total	221	2.25	.780		Total	221	2.56	.696
					Liking (Total)	J	94	28.53	4.357
						U −	51	29.82	3.598
						U +	35	31.31	2.805
						NS	41	31.83	3.368
						Total	221	29.88	4.007

Study 3 (Analysis 2) 67

Table 25. (continued)

Assertion Function-chain (results for test items)

		N	Mean	SD			N	Mean	SD
1a	J	94	2.96	.203	28a	J	94	2.23	.873
	U−	51	2.94	.311		U−	51	2.24	.862
	U+	35	2.94	.338		U+	35	2.29	.750
	NS	41	3.00	.000		NS	41	1.88	.872
	Total	221	2.96	.240		Total	221	2.18	.858
1b	J	94	2.99	.103	28b	J	94	2.43	.769
	U−	51	2.94	.238		U−	51	2.61	.723
	U+	35	2.94	.338		U+	35	2.66	.684
	NS	41	3.00	.000		NS	41	2.80	.459
	Total	221	2.97	.189		Total	221	2.57	.707
2a	J	94	2.27	.894	29a	J	94	2.09	.912
	U−	51	2.24	.839		U−	51	2.69	.616
	U+	35	2.23	.808		U+	35	2.89	.404
	NS	41	2.90	.374		NS	41	2.73	.593
	Total	221	2.37	.830		Total	221	2.47	.801
2b	J	94	2.40	.807	29b	J	94	2.39	.765
	U−	51	2.75	.560		U−	51	2.92	.337
	U+	35	2.91	.284		U+	35	2.89	.323
	NS	41	2.93	.346		NS	41	2.95	.312
	Total	221	2.66	.659		Total	221	2.70	.613
3a	J	94	2.91	.349	30a	J	94	2.13	.895
	U−	51	2.90	.413		U−	51	2.20	.917
	U+	35	2.94	.338		U+	35	2.23	.973
	NS	41	2.85	.422		NS	41	2.83	.495
	Total	221	2.90	.375		Total	221	2.29	.888
3b	J	94	2.72	.557	30b	J	94	2.41	.710
	U−	51	2.71	.576		U−	51	2.51	.784
	U+	35	2.77	.598		U+	35	2.60	.651
	NS	41	2.49	.810		NS	41	3.00	.000
	Total	221	2.68	.625		Total	221	2.57	.681
					Assertion (Total)	J	94	29.94	3.343
						U−	51	31.63	2.600
						U+	35	32.29	2.674
						NS	41	33.37	2.130
						Total	221	31.33	3.156

Reassurance Function-chain (results for test items)

		N	Mean	SD			N	Mean	SD
7a	J	94	2.87	.446	16a	J	94	2.59	.725
	U−	51	2.75	.627		U−	51	2.73	.493
	U+	35	2.94	.338		U+	35	2.86	.430
	NS	41	2.90	.300		NS	41	2.27	.837
	Total	221	2.86	.460		Total	221	2.60	.684
7b	J	94	2.81	.492	16b	J	94	2.60	.708
	U−	51	2.71	.672		U−	51	2.90	.413
	U+	35	2.89	.404		U+	35	3.00	.000
	NS	41	2.93	.264		NS	41	2.78	.571
	Total	221	2.82	.499		Total	221	2.76	.579
8a	J	94	2.05	.872	17a	J	94	2.46	.771
	U−	51	2.67	.653		U−	51	2.73	.603
	U+	35	2.91	.284		U+	35	2.94	.236
	NS	41	2.98	.156		NS	41	2.93	.346
	Total	221	2.50	.772		Total	221	2.68	.639
8b	J	94	2.35	.799	17b	J	94	2.21	.828
	U−	51	2.92	.337		U−	51	2.06	.810
	U+	35	2.97	.169		U+	35	2.46	.701
	NS	41	3.00	.000		NS	41	2.29	.844
	Total	221	2.70	.626		Total	221	2.23	.812
9a	J	94	2.70	.583	18a	J	94	2.84	.396
	U−	51	2.78	.541		U−	51	2.84	.464
	U+	35	2.97	.169		U+	35	2.94	.236
	NS	41	2.93	.264		NS	41	2.90	.300
	Total	221	2.81	.489		Total	221	2.87	.377
9b	J	94	2.83	.500	18b	J	94	2.98	.206
	U−	51	2.90	.413		U−	51	3.00	.000
	U+	35	2.97	.169		U+	35	3.00	.000
	NS	41	2.37	.859		NS	41	2.88	.331
	Total	221	2.78	.570		Total	221	2.97	.200
					Reassurance (Total)	J	94	31.29	3.463
						U−	51	32.98	2.421
						U+	35	34.86	1.287
						NS	41	33.15	2.565
						Total	221	32.59	3.080

68 A Study on the Acquisition of English Function-chains

Table 25. (continued)

Expressing Interest Function-chain (results for test items)

		N	Mean	SD		N	Mean	SD
4a	J	94	2.39	.806	25a	J	94	1.81	.895
	U−	51	2.73	.603		U−	51	1.94	.925
	U+	35	2.86	.494		U+	35	2.40	.812
	NS	41	2.85	.478		NS	41	2.95	.218
	Total	221	2.63	.693		Total	221	2.14	.913
4b	J	94	1.93	.883	25b	J	94	1.72	.860
	U−	51	2.24	.862		U−	51	1.88	.952
	U+	35	2.29	.860		U+	35	2.60	.775
	NS	41	2.07	.848		NS	41	2.78	.571
	Total	221	2.08	.875		Total	221	2.10	.932
5a	J	94	2.51	.744	26a	J	94	1.99	.810
	U−	51	2.88	.475		U−	51	1.69	.860
	U+	35	2.94	.236		U+	35	2.23	.877
	NS	41	2.93	.264		NS	41	2.80	.511
	Total	221	2.74	.589		Total	221	2.11	.867
5b	J	94	2.22	.882	26b	J	94	2.76	.581
	U−	51	2.41	.698		U−	51	2.65	.627
	U+	35	2.51	.742		U+	35	2.69	.676
	NS	41	1.95	.865		NS	41	2.98	.156
	Total	221	2.26	.833		Total	221	2.76	.565
6a	J	94	1.60	.807	27a	J	94	2.00	.916
	U−	51	1.63	.848		U−	51	1.86	.939
	U+	35	1.97	.857		U+	35	1.66	.873
	NS	41	2.73	.593		NS	41	1.76	.860
	Total	221	1.87	.896		Total	221	1.87	.908
6b	J	94	1.37	.762	27b	J	94	2.32	.751
	U−	51	1.39	.777		U−	51	2.57	.700
	U+	35	1.80	.901		U+	35	2.51	.702
	NS	41	2.12	.927		NS	41	2.71	.602
	Total	221	1.58	.868		Total	221	2.48	.717
					Interest (Total)	J	94	24.62	3.505
						U−	51	25.86	3.720
						U+	35	28.46	3.033
						NS	41	30.63	4.054
						Total	221	26.63	4.258

Table 26. Table of ANOVA

Assistance Function-chain ANOVA results

		SS	df	MS	F	p
13a	Between Groups	3.938	3	1.313	4.324	.006
	Within Groups	65.872	217	.304		
	Total	69.810	220			
13b	Between Groups	13.135	3	4.378	8.109	.000
	Within Groups	117.164	217	.540		
	Total	130.299	220			
14a	Between Groups	11.779	3	3.926	16.390	.000
	Within Groups	51.985	217	.240		
	Total	63.765	220			
14b	Between Groups	.620	3	.207	3.094	.028
	Within Groups	14.493	217	.067		
	Total	15.113	220			
15a	Between Groups	39.112	3	13.037	23.461	.000
	Within Groups	120.589	217	.556		
	Total	159.701	220			
15b	Between Groups	41.412	3	13.804	23.485	.000
	Within Groups	127.547	217	.588		
	Total	168.959	220			
22a	Between Groups	7.402	3	2.467	6.080	.001
	Within Groups	88.064	217	.406		
	Total	95.466	220			
22b	Between Groups	3.963	3	1.321	3.218	.024
	Within Groups	89.078	217	.410		
	Total	93.041	220			
23a	Between Groups	17.104	3	5.701	13.729	.000
	Within Groups	90.117	217	.415		
	Total	107.222	220			
23b	Between Groups	2.629	3	.876	4.582	.004
	Within Groups	41.506	217	.191		
	Total	44.136	220			
24a	Between Groups	3.697	3	1.232	2.910	.035
	Within Groups	91.878	217	.423		
	Total	95.575	220			
24b	Between Groups	3.771	3	1.257	6.243	.000
	Within Groups	43.687	217	.201		
	Total	47.457	220			
Assistance (Total)	Between Groups	789.778	3	263.259	29.866	.000
	Within Groups	1912.756	217	8.815		
	Total	2702.534	220			

Study 3 (Analysis 2)   69

Table 26. (continued)

Expressing Liking Function-chain results

		SS	df	MS	F	p
10a	Between Groups	8.287	3	2.762	7.007	.000
	Within Groups	85.541	217	.394		
	Total	93.828	220			
10b	Between Groups	2.691	3	.897	2.796	.041
	Within Groups	69.599	217	.321		
	Total	72.290	220			
11a	Between Groups	.285	3	.095	.139	.937
	Within Groups	148.719	217	.685		
	Total	149.005	220			
11b	Between Groups	16.736	3	5.579	15.406	.000
	Within Groups	78.576	217	.362		
	Total	95.312	220			
12a	Between Groups	.086	3	.029	.115	.951
	Within Groups	54.050	217	.249		
	Total	54.136	220			
12b	Between Groups	7.188	3	2.396	4.106	.007
	Within Groups	126.622	217	.584		
	Total	133.810	220			
19a	Between Groups	4.190	3	1.397	2.727	.045
	Within Groups	111.158	217	.512		
	Total	115.348	220			
19b	Between Groups	1.391	3	.464	3.753	.012
	Within Groups	26.799	217	.123		
	Total	28.190	220			
20a	Between Groups	8.896	3	2.965	3.868	.010
	Within Groups	166.344	217	.767		
	Total	175.240	220			
20b	Between Groups	15.531	3	5.177	10.652	.000
	Within Groups	105.464	217	.486		
	Total	120.995	220			
21a	Between Groups	9.424	3	3.141	4.358	.005
	Within Groups	156.413	217	.721		
	Total	165.837	220			
21b	Between Groups	15.565	3	5.188	12.375	.000
	Within Groups	90.978	217	.419		
	Total	106.543	220			
Liking (Total)	Between Groups	398.777	3	132.926	9.203	.000
	Within Groups	3134.164	217	14.443		
	Total	3532.941	220			

Assertion Function-chain results

		SS	df	MS	F	p
1a	Between Groups	.094	3	.031	.545	.652
	Within Groups	12.539	217	.058		
	Total	12.633	220			
1b	Between Groups	.138	3	.046	1.301	.275
	Within Groups	7.699	217	.035		
	Total	7.837	220			
2a	Between Groups	14.266	3	4.755	7.515	.000
	Within Groups	137.309	217	.633		
	Total	151.575	220			
2b	Between Groups	11.700	3	3.900	10.093	.000
	Within Groups	83.848	217	.386		
	Total	95.548	220			
3a	Between Groups	.168	3	.056	.394	.758
	Within Groups	30.837	217	.142		
	Total	31.005	220			
3b	Between Groups	2.016	3	.672	1.740	.160
	Within Groups	83.812	217	.386		
	Total	85.828	220			
28a	Between Groups	4.557	3	1.519	2.092	.102
	Within Groups	157.561	217	.726		
	Total	162.118	220			
28b	Between Groups	4.558	3	1.519	3.126	.027
	Within Groups	105.460	217	.486		
	Total	110.018	220			
29a	Between Groups	25.168	3	8.389	15.708	.000
	Within Groups	115.891	217	.534		
	Total	141.059	220			
29b	Between Groups	15.120	3	5.040	16.186	.000
	Within Groups	67.568	217	.311		
	Total	82.688	220			
30a	Between Groups	14.982	3	4.994	6.838	.000
	Within Groups	158.484	217	.730		
	Total	173.466	220			
30b	Between Groups	10.054	3	3.351	7.908	.000
	Within Groups	91.964	217	.424		
	Total	102.018	220			
Assertion (Total)	Between Groups	389.028	3	129.676	15.614	.000
	Within Groups	1802.194	217	8.305		
	Total	2191.222	220			

Table 26. (continued)

Reassurance Function-chain results

		SS	df	MS	F	p
7a	Between Groups	1.002	3	.334	1.587	.193
	Within Groups	45.650	217	.210		
	Total	46.652	220			
7b	Between Groups	1.295	3	.432	1.753	.157
	Within Groups	53.465	217	.246		
	Total	54.760	220			
8a	Between Groups	35.463	3	11.821	26.780	.000
	Within Groups	95.786	217	.441		
	Total	131.249	220			
8b	Between Groups	20.217	3	6.739	22.133	.000
	Within Groups	66.073	217	.304		
	Total	86.290	220			
9a	Between Groups	2.595	3	.865	3.751	.012
	Within Groups	50.039	217	.231		
	Total	52.633	220			
9b	Between Groups	9.305	3	3.102	10.808	.000
	Within Groups	62.270	217	.287		
	Total	71.575	220			
16a	Between Groups	7.649	3	2.550	5.805	.001
	Within Groups	95.311	217	.439		
	Total	102.959	220			
16b	Between Groups	5.592	3	1.864	5.934	.001
	Within Groups	68.172	217	.314		
	Total	73.765	220			
17a	Between Groups	9.675	3	3.225	8.731	.000
	Within Groups	80.153	217	.369		
	Total	89.828	220			
17b	Between Groups	3.489	3	1.163	1.781	.152
	Within Groups	141.742	217	.653		
	Total	145.231	220			
18a	Between Groups	.348	3	.116	.815	.487
	Within Groups	30.847	217	.142		
	Total	31.195	220			
18b	Between Groups	.431	3	.144	3.731	.012
	Within Groups	8.348	217	.038		
	Total	8.778	220			
Reassurance (Total)	Between Groups	359.897	3	119.966	15.068	.000
	Within Groups	1727.633	217	7.961		
	Total	2087.529	220			

Expressing Interest Function-chain results

		SS	df	MS	F	p
4a	Between Groups	9.574	3	3.191	7.214	.000
	Within Groups	96.001	217	.442		
	Total	105.575	220			
4b	Between Groups	4.955	3	1.652	2.191	.090
	Within Groups	163.579	217	.754		
	Total	168.534	220			
5a	Between Groups	8.849	3	2.950	9.490	.000
	Within Groups	67.450	217	.311		
	Total	76.299	220			
5b	Between Groups	7.472	3	2.491	3.719	.012
	Within Groups	145.307	217	.670		
	Total	152.778	220			
6a	Between Groups	40.872	3	13.624	21.806	.000
	Within Groups	135.580	217	.625		
	Total	176.452	220			
6b	Between Groups	19.586	3	6.529	9.696	.000
	Within Groups	146.115	217	.673		
	Total	165.701	220			
25a	Between Groups	41.687	3	13.896	21.283	.000
	Within Groups	141.679	217	.653		
	Total	183.367	220			
25b	Between Groups	43.478	3	14.493	21.317	.000
	Within Groups	147.527	217	.680		
	Total	191.005	220			
26a	Between Groups	30.813	3	10.271	16.561	.000
	Within Groups	134.580	217	.620		
	Total	165.394	220			
26b	Between Groups	2.752	3	.917	2.947	.034
	Within Groups	67.538	217	.311		
	Total	70.290	220			
27a	Between Groups	3.709	3	1.236	1.511	.212
	Within Groups	177.486	217	.818		
	Total	181.195	220			
27b	Between Groups	4.992	3	1.664	3.339	.020
	Within Groups	108.166	217	.498		
	Total	113.158	220			
Interest (Total)	Between Groups	1185.125	3	395.042	30.567	.000
	Within Groups	2804.450	217	12.924		
	Total	3989.575	220			

As Table 26 indicates, the difference between the levels of proficiency was shown to be statistically significant for the following test items at the .05 level — 13a, 13b, 14a, 14b, 15a, 15b, 22a, 22b, 23a, 23b, 24a, 24b, 10a, 10b, 11b, 12b, 19a, 19b, 20a, 20b, 21a, 21b, 2a, 2b, 28b, 29a, 29b, 30a, 30b, 8a, 8b, 9a, 9b, 16a, 16b, 17a, 18b, 4a, 5a, 5b, 6a, 6b, 25a, 25b, 26a, 26b, and 27b.

Table 27. Multiple comparisons of the levels of proficiency for each test item

Test item	Multiple comparisons	Test item	Multiple comparisons
13a	J < NS	28b	J < NS
13b	J ≒ U⁻ ≒ U⁺ < NS	29a	J < U⁻ ≒ U⁺ ≒ NS
14a	J ≒ U⁻ ≒ U⁺ > NS	29b	J < U⁻ ≒ U⁺ ≒ NS
14b	J < U⁻	30a	J ≒ U⁻ ≒ U⁺ < NS
15a	J < U⁻ ≒ U⁺ ≒ NS	30b	J ≒ U⁻ ≒ U⁺ < NS
15b	J < U⁻ < NS, J < U⁺	8a	J < U⁻ ≒ U⁺ ≒ NS
22a	J < NS	8b	J < U⁻ ≒ U⁺ ≒ NS
22b	J < NS	9a	J < U⁺
23a	J < U⁺ ≒ NS, U⁻ < NS	9b	J ≒ U⁻ ≒ U⁺ > NS
23b	J < U⁺ ≒ NS	16a	U⁻ ≒ U⁺ > NS
24a	J < U⁺	16b	J < U⁻ ≒ U⁺
24b	J < U⁻ ≒ U⁺ ≒ NS	17a	J < U⁺ ≒ NS
10a	J < U⁺ ≒ NS	18b	J ≒ U⁻ ≒ U⁺ > NS
10b	J < U⁺	4a	J < U⁻ ≒ U⁺ ≒ NS
11b	J < U⁻ ≒ U⁺ ≒ NS	5a	J < U⁻ ≒ U⁺ ≒ NS
12b	J > U⁻ ≒ NS	5b	U⁻ ≒ U⁺ > NS
19a	———	6a	J ≒ U⁻ ≒ U⁺ < NS
19b	J < U⁻	6b	J < U⁺ ≒ NS, U⁻ < NS
20a	J < NS	25a	J < U⁺ < NS, U⁻ < NS
20b	J < U⁺ ≒ NS, U⁻ < NS	25b	J ≒ U⁻ < U⁺ ≒ NS
21a	J ≒ U⁻ ≒ U⁺ < NS	26a	U⁻ < U⁺ ≒ NS, J < NS
21b	J < U⁻ ≒ NS, U⁺ < NS	26b	U⁻ < NS
2a	J ≒ U⁻ ≒ U⁺ < NS	27b	J < NS
2b	J < U⁻ ≒ U⁺ ≒ NS		

As for these significant test items, a post hoc analysis (Tukey's honestly significant difference test) was computed to study the differences between the means (the significance level was $p = .05$). For each item, multiple comparisons of the levels of proficiency yielded the results shown in Table 27 (see page 71). For the test item 19a, Table 26 showed that there was a significant difference between the levels of proficiency ($F (3, 217) = 2.727, p < .05$). However, the results of the post hoc analysis (Tukey's honestly significant difference test) showed no significant difference between any of the levels of proficiency at the .05 level.

From the results of the multiple comparisons of the levels of proficiency for each test item (Table 27), the items for which each group's scores were lower than those of native speakers were classified by the type of function-chains, the social relationship of the speakers, whether the responses were appropriate or inappropriate, and then made into a table (see Table 28-1). Table 28-2 shows the specific function-chains from Table 28-1. These items can be regarded as the areas of difficulty specific to each group.

In Table 28-1, the items enclosed by a square (☐) are those for which scores were lower than those of native speakers, irrespective of English proficiency level.

The items for which the scores of the Japanese students (in one or more of the study groups) were statistically higher than those of native speakers were also classified and put into a table in the same manner (see Table 29-1). For these six items in Table 29-1, the group scores of some of the Japanese students were statistically higher than those of native speakers. However, it should be noted that even among the native speakers, the participants who judged these items correctly as inappropriate outnumbered those who judged these items to be "neither" or "appropriate." Therefore, we can say that the general (continued on p.77)

Study 3 (Analysis 2) 73

Table 28-1. Function-chains for which scores are lower than those of native speakers (revealing areas of difficulty specific to each group)

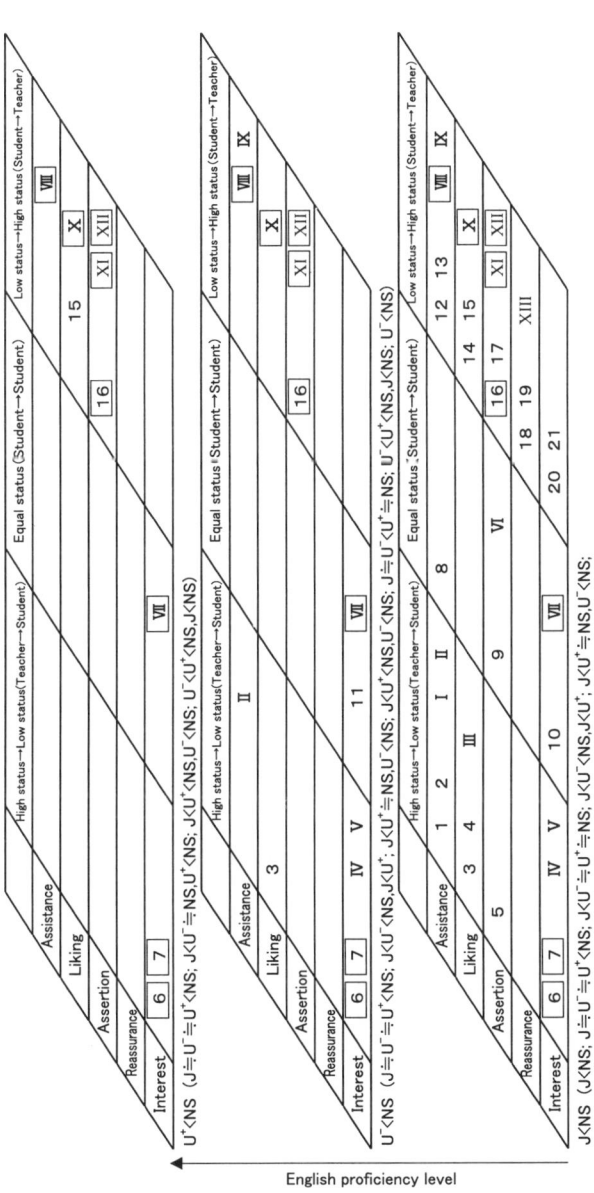

[Table content - three stacked grid panels showing function-chains by English proficiency level]

Panel 1 (top, highest proficiency):
- Columns: Assistance, Liking, Assertion, Reassurance, Interest
- Rows: High status→Low status (Teacher→Student); Equal status (Student↔Student); Low status→High status (Student→Teacher)
- Entries: 6, 7 under Interest/Assertion; VII; 15 / 16; VIII, X, XI, XII

$U^+ < NS$ (J≒U⁻≒U⁺<NS; J<U⁺<NS,U⁻<NS; U⁻<U⁺<NS,J<NS)

Panel 2 (middle):
- Entries: 6, 7; 3; II; VII; 11; 16; VIII, IX, X, XI, XII

$U^- < NS$ (J≒U⁻≒U⁺<NS; J<U⁺<NS,J<U⁺; J<U⁺≒NS,U⁻<NS; J<U⁺<NS,U⁻<NS; J≒U⁻<U⁺≒NS: U⁻<U⁺<NS,J<NS: U⁻<NS)

Panel 3 (bottom, lowest proficiency):
- Entries: 1, 2, I, II, 8; 3, 4, III; 5, IV, V, 9, VI; 6, 10; 7, VII; 12, 13, 14, 15, 16, 17, 18, 19, 20, 21, VIII, IX, X, XI, XII, XIII

J<NS (J<NS; J≒U⁻≒U⁺<NS; J<U⁺<NS,J<U⁺; J<U⁺≒NS,U⁻<NS; J<U⁺≒NS; J<U⁺≒NS,U⁻<NS; J≒U⁻<U⁺≒NS; U⁻<U⁺≒NS; U⁻<NS,J<NS)

English proficiency level ←

Arabic numerals (e.g., 1, 2, 3,...21): Appropriate statements
Roman numerals (e.g., I, II, III, ...XIII): Inappropriate statements
☐ : Function-chains for which scores were lower than those of native speakers irrespective of English proficiency

NS : Native speakers
U⁺ : Japanese university students with experience of study abroad
U⁻ : Japanese university students w/o experience of study abroad
J : Japanese junior high school students

Table 28-2. Specific function-chains from Table 28-1 that proved difficult for Japanese EFL learners

	High status→Low status (Teacher→Student)	Equal status (Student → Student)	Low status→High status (Student→Teacher)
Assistance	(1) Will you help me? → Of course. (J < U⁻ ≒ U⁺ ≒ NS) (2) Will you help me? → Sure, I can handle that. (J < NS) (I) Will you help me? → I guess I will if you can't do it yourself. (J < NS) (II) Will you help me? → Yes, if I have to. (J < U⁺ < NS, J < U⁺)	(8) Will you help me? → No problem. (J < U⁻ ≒ U⁺ ≒ NS)	(12) Will you help me? → Sure. (J < U⁺ ≒ NS) (13) Will you help me? → Certainly. (J < NS) (VIII) Will you help me? → Yeah, why not? (J ≒ U⁻ ≒ U⁺ < NS) (IX) Will you help me? → I guess so. (J < U⁺ ≒ NS, U⁻ < NS)
Liking	(3) Do you like ice skating? → Yes, I really enjoy it. (J < U⁺ ≒ NS, U⁻ < NS) (4) Do you like this costume? → It's great! (J < U⁺ ≒ NS) (III) Do you like ice skating? → It is simply the most divine activity I have ever done. (J < NS)		(14) Do you like this costume? → Yes, I really like it. (J < U⁻ ≒ U⁺ ≒ NS) (15) Do you like ice skating? → Yes, I do. (J < U⁻ ≒ NS, U⁺ < NS) (X) Do you like ice skating? → Yeah, ice skating is totally awesome. It's so cool, you know. (J ≒ U⁻ ≒ U⁺ < NS)
Assertion	(5) Do you think we need another parking area? → Yes, we certainly do. (J < NS)	(9) Do you think we need another parking area? → Yes, I do. (J < U⁻ ≒ U⁺ ≒ NS) (VI) Do you think we need another parking area? → That is my conviction. (J < U⁻ ≒ U⁺ ≒ NS)	(16) Do you think we need another parking area? → Yes, we do. (J ≒ U⁻ ≒ U⁺ < NS) (17) Do you think we need computers? → Yes, they're very useful. (J < U⁻ ≒ U⁺ ≒ NS) (XI) Do you think we need computers? → That's obvious, isn't it?

Study 3 (Analysis 2)   75

	Appropriate	Inappropriate
Reassurance		(XII) Do you think we need another parking area? → Yeah, we totally need a new parking area, man. (J ≒ U⁻ ≒ U⁺ < NS) (18) I don't understand what you mean. → OK, let me explain in a different way. (J < U⁻ ≒ U⁺ ≒ NS) (19) Excuse me. The computer isn't working well. → Don't worry about it. I can fix it. (J < U⁺ ≒ NS) (XIII) I don't understand what you mean. → Let me explain so that any child can understand. (J < U⁻ ≒ U⁺ ≒ NS) (20) I stayed in Canada last summer. → Did you enjoy it? (J < U⁻ ≒ U⁺ ≒ NS) (21) I went to Disneyland this weekend. → That sounds like fun. (J < NS)
Interest	(6) I stayed in Canada last summer. → What did you do there? (J ≒ U⁻ ≒ U⁺ < NS) (7) I went to Disneyland this weekend. → How was it? (J < U⁺ < NS, U⁻ < NS) (IV) I stayed in Canada last summer. → Would you be so kind to tell me more? (J < U⁺ ≒ NS, U⁻ < NS) (V) I went to Disneyland this weekend. → Oh, tell me every little detail. I can't wait to hear. (J ≒ U⁻ < U⁺ ≒ NS)	(10) I stayed in Canada last summer. → Did you do anything fun? (J < U⁻ ≒ U⁺ ≒ NS) (11) I went to Disneyland this weekend. → Lucky you! (U⁻ < NS) (VII) I went to Disneyland this weekend. → Indeed? (U⁻ < U⁺ < NS, J < NS)

Arabic numerals (e.g. 1, 2, 3, ...21): Appropriate statements
Roman numerals (e.g. I, II, III, ...XIII): Inappropriate statements

Table 29-1. Function-chains for which scores are higher than those of native speakers

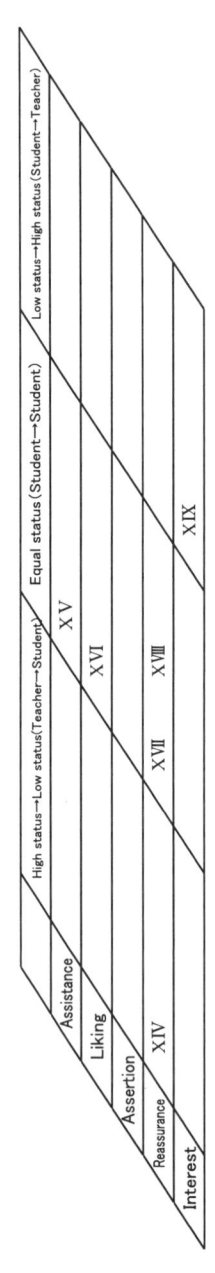

	High status→Low status (Teacher→Student)	Equal status (Student→Student)	Low status→High status (Student→Teacher)
Assistance		XV	
Liking		XVI	
Assertion		XVII	XVIII
Reassurance	XIV		
Interest			XIX

Roman numerals (e.g. XIV, XV, ...XIX): Inappropriate statements

Table 29-2. Specific function-chains from Table 29-1

XIV: Well, the computer isn't working well. → Now, now, take it easy. ($J \fallingdotseq U^- \fallingdotseq U^+ > NS$)
XV: Will you help me? → I would be glad to offer you assistance. ($J \fallingdotseq U^- \fallingdotseq U^+ > NS$)
XVI: Do you like this costume? → Yes, your costume is very nicely made. ($J > U^- \fallingdotseq NS$)
XVII: Well, the computer isn't working well.
 → Allow me to troubleshoot your machine and I will have it running perfectly. ($U^- \fallingdotseq U^+ > NS$)
XVIII: I don't understand what you mean. → Please allow me to explain again. ($J \fallingdotseq U^- \fallingdotseq U^+ > NS$)
XIX: I stayed in Canada last summer. → Really, I would give anything for a chance to go to Canada. ($U^- \fallingdotseq U^+ > NS$)

tendency of their judgment coincided with the test preparers' collective judgment. Table 29-2 shows the specific function-chains from Table 29-1.

Using these tables, we will look for specific patterns of similarities and differences, and go on to identify the following three characteristics of Japanese students in the discussion section: 1) the areas of difficulty specific to each group; 2) those areas difficult for Japanese EFL learners irrespective of English proficiency level; and 3) the areas in which Japanese EFL learners were over-sensitive (overly strict) in their judgment as to what constituted appropriate language.

6.4 Discussion

The first point to be discussed examines the areas of difficulty specific to each group.

First, the items for which junior high school students' scores were lower than native speakers ($J < NS$; $J \fallingdotseq U^- \fallingdotseq U^+ < NS$; $J < U^- \fallingdotseq U^+ \fallingdotseq NS$; $J < U^- < NS$, $J < U^+$; $J < U^+ \fallingdotseq NS$, $U^- < NS$; $J < U^+ \fallingdotseq NS$; $J < U^- \fallingdotseq NS$, $U^+ < NS$; $J < U^+ < NS$, $U^- < NS$; $J \fallingdotseq U^- < U^+ \fallingdotseq NS$; $U^- < U^+ < NS$, $J < NS$) were classified by the type of function-chains, the social relationship of the speakers, whether the responses were appropriate or inappropriate, and then made into a table (Table 28-1). These items can be regarded as the areas of difficulty specific to junior high school students. When we examine this table (see Table 28-2), the following two points were found to be characteristic of Japanese junior high school students: (1) As a whole their scores for both appropriate and inappropriate responses are lower than those of native speakers. For example, they judge even typical responses, such as <u>Will you help me?</u> → <u>No problem.</u>, <u>Do you like this costume?</u> → <u>Yes, I really like it.</u>, and <u>Do you think we need another parking area?</u> → <u>Yes, I</u>

do., to be inappropriate. (2) Generally they have more difficulty rendering a correct judgment for dialogues between people of low status and high status, as compared to dialogues between equals. One explanation for this may be that dialogues in the English textbooks used in Japan are between equals for the most part, meaning that there are relatively few exercises where age or status differences come into play, as Fukazawa (1997, 2000) points out.

The items for which the scores of the U^- students were lower than native speakers ($J \fallingdotseq U^- \fallingdotseq U^+ < NS$; $J < U^- < NS$, $J < U^+$; $J < U^+ \fallingdotseq NS$, $U^- < NS$; $J < U^+ < NS$, $U^- < NS$; $J \fallingdotseq U^- < U^+ \fallingdotseq NS$; $U^- < U^+ < NS$, $J < NS$; $U^- < NS$) were classified and put into a table in the same manner as the results of the junior high school students (Table 28-1). These items can be regarded as the areas of difficulty specific to the U^- students. The following five points were found to be characteristic of this group when compared to the junior high school students: (1) They were able to judge correctly many of the typical responses as being appropriate, while junior high school students could not. (2) They successfully recognized the inappropriateness of teachers' sarcastic remarks to students, such as I don't understand what you mean. → Let me explain so that any child can understand. (3) They were able to judge the inappropriateness of students' expressing liking to a teacher in too flowery a tone, for example, Do you like ice skating? → It is simply the most divine activity I have ever done., and also the inappropriateness of students' showing an inconsiderate and disrespectful attitude towards a teacher when offering assistance, such as Will you help me? → I guess I will if you can't do it yourself. (4) They could recognize the inappropriateness of assertions made in too formal a manner between close friends, such as, Do you think we need another parking area? → That is my conviction. (5) They had some trouble rendering a correct judgment concerning dialogues between those of low status and high status, as compared to dialogues between equals. But overall, they did better than junior high school students in this area.

The items for which the scores of the U^+ students were lower than native speakers ($J \fallingdotseq U^- \fallingdotseq U^+ <$ NS; $J < U^- \fallingdotseq$ NS, $U^+ <$ NS; $J < U^+ <$ NS, $U^- <$ NS; $U^- < U^+ <$ NS, $J <$ NS) were classified and put into a table in a like manner as the other two groups of students (Table 28-1). These items can be regarded as the areas of difficulty specific to the U^+ students. When compared to the U^- students, the following three points were found to be characteristic of this group: (1) They successfully recognized as inappropriate certain function-chains expressing reluctance to offer assistance, such as Will you help me? → Yes, if I have to., and Will you help me? → I guess so. (2) They recognized the inappropriateness of too flowery and formal remarks made by students to teachers, such as I stayed in Canada last summer. → Would you be so kind to tell me more? Also they recognized the inappropriateness of remarks of students to teachers showing an overdone and perhaps insincere interest, such as I went to Disneyland this weekend. → Oh, tell me every little detail. I can't wait to hear. (3) In general, low status to high status dialogues proved to be the most difficult for U^+ students, while they did well with high status to low status dialogues as compared to students in the other two groups. That is, it was difficult for them to judge the appropriateness of teachers' replies to students' utterances, while based on their experience as students it was relatively easier for them to judge students' replies to teachers.

Next, let us investigate the areas difficult for Japanese EFL learners irrespective of English proficiency level. In Table 28-1, the items enclosed by a square (□) are those for which scores were lower than those of native speakers irrespective of English proficiency. When we examine these items (see Table 28-2), they were found to exhibit the following four characteristics: (1) Japanese students regard as acceptable too hip or sarcastic remarks made by teachers to students, such as Will you help me? → Yeah, why not?, Do you like ice skating? → Yeah, ice skating is totally awesome. It's so cool, you know., Do you think we need computers? → That's obvious, isn't it?, and Do you think we need another parking area? → Yeah, we totally need a new parking area, man. (2) Japanese students regard as inappropriate students' expressions of direct interest to teachers' remarks, such as I stayed in Canada last summer. → What did you do there?, and I went to Disneyland this weekend. → How was it? (3) It is difficult for Japanese students to judge whether the use of the interjection "indeed" is appropriate or not according to the situation, such as I went to Disneyland this weekend. → Indeed? (4) It is difficult for Japanese students to recognize as appropriate teachers' positive polite assertion, such as Do you think we need another parking area? → Yes, we do.

Finally, let us consider the areas in which Japanese EFL learners were over-sensitive in their judgment. The items for which at least some of the Japanese group scores were statistically higher than those of native speakers (J ≑ U⁻ ≑ U⁺ > NS; J > U⁻ ≑ NS; U⁻ ≑ U⁺ > NS) were classified by the type of function-chains, the social relationship of the speakers, whether the responses were appropriate or inappropriate, and then made into a table (Table 29-1). These six items were all inappropriate responses; therefore, we can say that Japanese students judged these items to be inappropriate in a stricter manner than the native speakers from the United States. It may be the case that even among native speakers there are those who are relatively liberal in their speech standards, and thus likely to tolerate non-standard usage. When we examine this table (see Table 29-2), the following three points were found to be characteristic of these items: (1) When compared to native speakers, their judgment is more strict as to what constitutes too formal and polite remarks between friends, such as Will you help me? → I would be glad to offer you assistance., Do you like this costume? → Yes, your costume is very nicely made., Well, the computer isn't working well. → Allow me to troubleshoot your machine and I will have it running perfectly., and I don't understand what you mean. → Please allow me to explain again. (2) They judge a reassuring response by a student to a teacher, such as Well, the computer isn't working well. → Now, now, take it easy., to be inappropriate more strictly than native speakers. (3) They also judge a teacher expressing interest too dramatically to a student, such as I stayed in Canada last summer. → Really, I would give anything for a chance to go to Canada., to be inappropriate more strictly than native speakers.

It might be the case that these are function-chains where judgment of appropriateness is affected by cultural background or values. A recommendation of how this issue might be dealt with will be presented in the following chapter, which offers the conclusions of this paper and remaining problems.

Notes

[1] With the increasing acceptance of qualitative research in education, many researchers who conduct L2 research in classrooms and schools have become interested in the ways in which qualitative studies can inform the SLA field (Davis, 1995). Lazaraton (1995) reviews the role of quantification in qualitative research and the generalizability of qualitative research.

[2] Using matrices to describe and analyze qualitative data was widespread in the field of error analysis, especially during the 1970s. For example, Corder (1973) designed a classified table for errors, which has two dimensions, with one set of

categories labeled across the top (phonological/orthographical, grammatical, and lexical) and another down the left-hand side (omission, addition, selection, ordering). Brown (1980) also designed the categories for errors, which adds a dimension for systematicity of errors (Ozasa (ed), 1983). As for the interpretation of the matrices, Lynch (1992) used the following techniques: (1) scan for general patterns, (2) peruse the data for more specific difference patterns, (3) look for specific similarity patterns, (4) check for predominant outcomes, and (5) examine the data for repeating or overlapping elements. Following Lynch's techniques, the present study attempts to find interesting and useful patterns in the data.

Chapter 7
Conclusions and remaining problems

7.1 Conclusions and pedagogical implications

In this thesis, the following two main points were investigated: 1) the relationships between the function-chains used as the test items in this study, and the relation between the patterns found and the junior high school students' judgment as regards textual appropriateness, and 2) the effect of the level of proficiency in English and the type of function-chains on the ability of students to recognize social and stylistic appropriateness.

The findings of this investigation can be summarized as follows.

First, the factors which best explained the relation between the function-chains and the students' judgment were extracted by using factor analysis. The factors were inferred to be as follows: asking or giving one's opinion" (Factor 1), "expressing surprise or excitement" (Factor 2), and "expressing displeasure" (Factor 3). Hayashi's quantification model III was also used, and the two dimensions (Dimension I and Dimension II) were extracted. In this study Dimension I was interpreted to be the axis that meant "satire and scorn" and Dimension II was interpreted as the axis signifying "inventiveness in communication." From this study we found that various patterns or factors were involved in the junior high school students' judgment regarding the function-chains from the scripted speech. On the other hand, the variation of students' judgment concerning the function-chains from English textbooks was smaller than that from the scripted speech. That is, as a whole the junior high school students reached similar judgments on the function-chains from English textbooks. Hence, we can say that the students have different attitudes towards the function-chains from the scripted speech and the function-chains from English textbooks.

Second, to investigate the effect of the level of proficiency in English and the type of function-chains on the ability to recognize appropriateness, two studies (Studies 2 and 3) were conducted. Study 2 divided Japanese junior high school students into two groups (a relatively high proficiency group and a low proficiency group) according to their English proficiency level, and then investigated the relation between proficiency and pragmatic development. As a result, it was found that the students with high English proficiency achieve higher levels of recognition of appropriateness as regards function-chains. As for the type of function-chains, for the Expressing Liking Function-chain and the Assertion Function-chain, there was a significant difference between the levels of proficiency in English, with the relatively high proficiency group's score being higher than the low proficiency group's. It suggests that as students gain English proficiency they find it increasingly easy to identify appropriateness in these types of function-chain. Study 3 also investigated the relation between proficiency and pragmatic development. This study extended the range of participants and compared the following groups: J, U^-, U^+, and NS. As a result, the four study groups, representing different levels of English proficiency, did show a statistically significant difference in their recognition of the appropriateness of the five types of function-chains used in the test. However, depending on the type of function-chain involved, the amount of improvement, as regards recognition of appropriateness between levels of English proficiency, varied considerably. That is to say, each function-chain shows its own unique rate and route of development for the study groups involved. As for the relative level of difficulty of the types of function-chains, different types of function-chains presented an almost equal level of difficulty for the Japanese students. For native speakers, however, some types of function-chains presented distinctly different levels of difficulty. This differentiation of the relative level of difficulty seems to suggest a direction of language acquisition. Further, qualitative analysis was employed along with the quantitative results, and the following characteristics of Japanese students were identified when compared to native speakers: the areas of difficulty specific to each group, those areas difficult for Japanese EFL learners irrespective of English proficiency level, and the areas in which Japanese EFL learners scored better than native speakers in their judgment as to what constituted appropriate language.

As for the pedagogical implications, we can present the following four points.

First, function-chains possessing similar characteristics can be grouped together for ease of presentation and understanding. Also, by plotting function-chains on a graph, we can clarify the relationships among them. So, when teachers design lessons and everyday practices for their classrooms with a focus on language functions, they can group the function-chains with common features together, and thus present them to students more effectively.

Second, it was found that each type of function-chain shows its own unique rate and route of development for certain learners. Based on this information, teachers can have a vision of how the learners' recognition of appropriateness for each type of function-chain will improve as they gain English proficiency.

Third, the construction of a scale identifying the relative level of difficulty of function-chains provides information that may be useful for future program design — what sort of function-chains should be given priority when they are taught.

Fourth, in this study, the areas of difficulty specific to each group were identified. These areas of difficulty can be interpreted as areas requiring more in-depth instruction. If these areas were consciously focused on while teaching to each group, it could be hoped that the students of each group would gain a better understanding as to what constitutes appropriate language. The areas of difficulty for Japanese EFL learners irrespective of English proficiency level were also identified. We need to take these areas into consideration when editing teaching materials and preparing classroom activities. At the same time, this study revealed not only these areas of difficulty, but also areas of relative success in the acquisition process. It became clear that learners can be successful in certain areas of pragmatics.

7.2 The remaining problems and implications for future research

Thus far we have summarized the conclusions and pedagogical implications of this study. However, there are still some questions requiring further discussion.

First, in Study 1, factor analysis was applied to the results of the junior high school students' judgment, and then the three factors were extracted which best explained the relation between the function-chains and the students' judgment. The author interpreted the three factors based on the factor loadings. However, we should take further steps to check the reliability of this interpretation of these three factors. That is, we should pick out the items relevant to the factors, and then analyze the judgment of the students once again. Hayashi's quantification model III was also used, and the two dimensions (Dimension I and Dimension II) were extracted.

The author interpreted Dimension I and Dimension II by the features of the function-chains whose category scores were high. However, the eigenvalues of Dimension I and Dimension II did not seem to be high enough to explain the variance in the participants' judgment. Further, as there was no hypothesis made beforehand, each dimension's results should be considered as tentative at best. The author suggests that multivariate analysis with more appropriate data could be used as a method to yield more significant information.

Second, in Studies 2 and 3, the appropriateness judgment tests were developed by several American residents teaching in Japan. They verified that the test items in each function-chain were classified correctly as regarding the type of function-chain involved. They were also in full agreement as to the ratings of appropriateness. Therefore, these tests were used as a yardstick to assess the participants' pragmatic competence. However, it can be questioned whether the test preparers' judgments would be consistent enough, and reliable enough, to function as an absolute yardstick in all circumstances. Judgment of appropriateness is a delicate matter. We will always encounter difficulties when trying to prepare absolutely appropriate utterances or absolutely inappropriate utterances as test items for pragmatic assessment. The possibility of variance in judgment as to what constitutes appropriateness, even among native speakers, is a real problem for which we have to seek a solution when establishing any standard to assess pragmatic competence. Thus, it is recommendable that steps be taken to check and improve the reliability of any future appropriateness judgment test. The quality of the test preparers, the procedures employed in making and administering the test, as well as the selection of those who will take the test, are all areas that must be done with the utmost care. The results obtained from such a test could then be compared with the results of this study in order to confirm its conclusions.

Third, as respects those function-chains where judgment of appropriateness may be influenced by cultural background or values, including those areas for which Japanese EFL learners were over-sensitive in their judgment, in-depth investigation, such as carrying out personal interviews with study participants, could give us valuable insights. Additionally, cooperative research with the Japanese education field concerning the above points is recommendable, as it could shed further light on this issue.

Finally, this set of studies provides information about participants' perception and comprehension of speech act realizations. A foreseeable extension of this research would be to include a study that analyzes the appropriateness of participants' actual speech production, in addition to the areas mentioned above. Such study, encompassing both perception and production procedures, should yield comprehensive information on the manner in which Japanese EFL learners acquire pragmatic competence.

Thus, these studies require further empirical scrutiny. However, despite its limitations, the author hopes that the findings of this thesis will help to shed light on certain aspects of learners' pragmatic competence to recognize the appropriateness of written and spoken English in the particular settings in which it is used. If it has accomplished that, this thesis should provide a modest but useful contribution to English language teaching.

References

Bachman, L. (1990). *Fundamental considerations in language testing.* Oxford: Oxford University Press.

Bachman, L., & Palmer, A. (1996). *Language testing in practice: Designing and developing useful language tests.* Oxford: Oxford University Press.

Bardovi-Harlig, K. (1999). Exploring the interlanguage of interlanguage pragmatics: A research agenda for acquisitional pragmatics. *Language Learning, 49,* 677-713.

Bardovi-Harlig, K. (2001). Evaluating the empirical evidence. In K. Rose & G. Kasper (Eds.), *Pragmatics in language teaching* (pp. 13-32). Cambridge: Cambridge University Press.

Bardovi-Harlig, K., & Hartford, B. S. (1993). Learning the rules of academic talk: A longitudinal study of pragmatic development. *Studies in Second Language Acquisition, 15,* 279-304.

Billmyer, K. (1990a) *The effect of formal instruction on the development of sociolinguistic competence: The performance of compliments.* Unpublished doctoral dissertation, University of Pennsylvania, Philadelphia.

Billmyer, K. (1990b). "I really like your lifestyle": ESL learners learning how to compliment. *Penn Working Papers in Educational Linguistics, 6,* 31-48.

Blum-Kulka, S., House, J., & Kasper, G. (1989). The CCSARP coding manual. In S. Blum-Kulka, J. House & G. Kasper (Eds.), *Cross-cultural pragmatics: Requests and apologies* (pp. 273-294). Norwood, NJ: Ablex.

Blum-Kulka, S., & Olshtain, E. (1986). Too many words: Length of utterance and pragmatic failure. *Studies in Second Language Acquisition, 8,* 47-61.

Blundell, J., Higgens, J., & Middlemiss, N. (1982). *Function in English.* Oxford: Oxford University Press.

Bouton, L. F. (1992). The interpretation of implicature in English by NNS: Does it come automatically — without being explicitly taught? In L. F. Bouton & Y. Kachru (Eds.), *Pragmatics and language learning* (Vol. 3, pp. 53-65). Urbana-Champaign: University of Illinois, Division of English as an International Language.

Brown, H. D. (1980). *Principles of language learning and teaching.* Englewood Cliffs: Prentice-Hall, Inc.

Campbell, R., & Wales, R. (1970). The study of language acquisition. In J. Lyons (Ed.), *New horizons in linguistics* (pp. 242-260). Harmondsworth: Penguin.

Canale, M. (1983). From communicative competence to language pedagogy. In J. Richards & R. Schmidt (Eds.), *Language and communication* (pp. 2-27). London: Longman.

Canale, M., & Swain, M. (1980). Theoretical bases of communicative approaches to second language teaching and testing. *Applied Linguistics, 1,* 1-47.

Carrell, P. L., & Konneker, B. H. (1981). Politeness: Comparing native and nonnative

judgments. *Language Learning, 31*, 17-31.
Cook, V. (1991). *Second language learning and language teaching*. London: Edward Arnold.
Cook, V. (1993). *Linguistics and second language acquisition*. New York: St. Martin's Press.
Corder, S. P. (1973). *Introducing applied linguistics*. Harmondsworth: Penguin Books.
Davices, J.H. (Producer). (1975). *The good life* [Television series]. BBC.
Davis, K. A. (1995). Qualitative theory and methods in applied linguistics research. *TESOL Quarterly, 29*, 427-453.
Ellis, R. (1992). Learning to communicate in the classroom: A study of two language learners' requests. *Studies in Second Language Acquisition, 14*, 1-23.
Finocchiaro, M., & Brumfit, C. (1983). *The functional-notional approach from theory to practice*. Oxford: Oxford University Press.
Fukazawa, S. (2003). A study of the development of pragmatic competence by Japanese learners of English. *ARELE, 14*, 11-20.
Fukazawa, S., & Sasaki, T. (2004). Use of supportive moves in interlanguage requests in English as a foreign language. *JABAET Journal, 8*, 5-19.
Ginn, S.B. (1996). *World of language teacher edition K*. Needham Heights, MA: Silver Burdett Ginn.
Guntermann, G. (1979). Developing functional proficiency in a foreign language. *Foreign Language Annals, 12*, 219-225.
Halliday, M. A. K. (1973). *Explorations in the functions of language*. London: Edward Arnold.
Holmes, J., & Brown, D. (1987). Teachers and students learning about compliments. *TESOL Quarterly, 21*, 523-546.
Hymes, D. (1972). On communicative competence. In J. Pride & J. Holmes (Eds.), *Sociolinguistics: Selected readings* (pp. 269-293). Harmondsworth: Penguin.
Kasper, G. (1981). *Pragmatische Aspekte in der Interimsprache* [Pragmatic aspects of interlanguage]. Tübingen: Narr.
Kasper, G. (1992). Pragmatic transfer. *Second Language Research, 8*, 203-231.
Kasper, G., & Dahl, M. (1991). Research methods in interlanguage pragmatics. *Studies in Second Language Acquisition, 13*, 215-247.
Kasper, G., & Rose, K. (2001). Pragmatics in language teaching. In K. Rose & G. Kasper (Eds.), *Pragmatics in language teaching* (pp. 1-12). Cambridge: Cambridge University Press.
Kasper, G., & Schmidt, R. (1996). Developmental issues in interlanguage pragmatics. *Studies in Second Language Acquisition, 18*, 149-169.
Kerekes, J. (1992). *Development in nonnative speakers' use and perceptions of assertiveness and supportiveness in a mixed-sex conversation* (Occasional Paper No.21). Honolulu: University of Hawai'i at Manoa, Department of English as a Second Language.

Lazaraton, A. (1995). Qualitative research in applied linguistics: A progress report. *TESOL Quarterly, 29*, 455-472.

Lynch, B. (1992). Evaluating a program inside and out. In J. C. Alderson & A. Beretta (Eds.), *Evaluating second language education*. Cambridge, England: Cambridge University Press.

Maeshiba, N., Yoshinaga, N., Kasper, G., & Ross, S. (1996). Transfer and proficiency in interlanguage apologizing. In S. Gass & J. Neu (Eds.), *Speech acts across cultures* (pp. 155-187). Berlin: Mouton de Gruyter.

Matsumura, S. (2001). Learning the rules for offering advice: A quantitative approach to second language socialization. *Language Learning, 51*, 635-679.

Matsumura, S. (2003). Modelling the relationships among interlanguage pragmatic development, L2 proficiency, and exposure to L2. *Applied Linguistics, 24*, 465-491.

McCarthy, M. (1991). *Discourse analysis for language teachers*. Cambridge: Cambridge University Press.

Murphy, B., & Neu, J. (1996). My grade's too low: The speech act set of complaining. In S. M. Gass & J. Neu (Eds.), *Speech acts across cultures: Challenge to communication in a second language* (pp. 191-216). Berlin: Mouton de Gruyter.

Niezgoda, K., & Röver, C. (2001). Pragmatic and grammatical awareness: A function of the learning environment? In K. Rose & G. Kasper (Eds.), *Pragmatics in language teaching* (pp. 63-79). Cambridge: Cambridge University Press.

Olshtain, E., & Blum-Kulka, S. (1985). Degree of approximation: Nonnative reactions to native speech act behavior. In S.M. Gass & C. Madden (Eds.), *Input in second language acquisition* (pp. 303-325). Rowley, MA: Newbury House.

Olshtain, E., & Cohen, A. (1983). Apology: A speech act set. In N. Wolfson & E. Judd (Eds.), *Sociolinguistics and second language acquisition* (pp. 18-35). New York: Newbury House.

Omar, A.S. (1991). How learners greet in Kiswahili. In L.Bouton & Y. Kachru (Eds.), *Pragmatics and language learning* (Vol. 2, pp. 59-73). Urbana-Champaign: University of Illinois, Division of English as an International Language.

Papalia, A. (1982). Developing communication skills in the second language classroom: A preliminary report. *The Canadian Modern Language Review, 38*, 685-688.

Richards, J. C., & Schmidt, R. (2002). *Longman dictionary of language teaching and applied linguistics*. London: Longman.

Rintell, E. (1984). But how did you feel about that? The learner's perception of emotion in speech. *Applied Linguistics, 5*, 255-264.

Robinson, M. A. (1992). Introspective methodology in interlanguage pragmatics research. In G. Kasper (Ed.), *Pragmatics of Japanese as a native and target language* (Tech. Rep. No. 3, pp. 27-82). Honolulu: University of Hawai'i at Manoa, Second Language Teaching and Curriculum Center.

Rose, K. (2000). An exploratory cross-sectional study of interlanguage pragmatic development. *Studies in Second Language Acquisition, 22*, 27-67.

Sawyer, M. (1992). The development of pragmatics in Japanese as a second language: The sentence-final particle *ne*. In G. Kasper (Ed.), *Pragmatics of Japanese as a native and foreign language* (Tech. Rep. No. 3, pp. 83-125). Honolulu: University of Hawai'i at Manoa, Second Language Teaching and Curriculum Center.

Scarcella, R. (1979). On speaking politely in a second language. In C.A.Yorio, K. Perkins, & J. Schachter (Eds.), *On TESOL '79* (pp. 275-287). Washington, DC: TESOL.

Schmidt, R. (1983). Interaction, acculturation, and the acquisition of communicative competence: A case study of an adult. In E. Judd & N. Wolfson (Eds.), *Sociolinguistics and language acquisition* (pp. 137-174). Rowley, MA: Newbury House.

Schmidt, R., & Frota, S. N. (1986). Developing basic conversational ability in a second language: A case study of a learner of Portuguese. In R. Day (Ed.), *Talking to learn* (pp. 237-326). Rowley, MA: Newbury House.

Scollon, R., & Scollon, S.W. (2001). *Intercultural communication*. Oxford, UK: Blackwell.

Siegal, M. (1994). *Looking East: Learning Japanese as a second language in Japan and the interaction of race, gender and social context*. Unpublished doctoral dissertation, University of California, Berkeley.

Svanes, B. (1992). En undersoekelse av realisasjonsmoenstret for spraakhandlingen "aa be noen om aa gjoere noe" [An investigation of the realization pattern of linguistic action "to ask someone to do something"]. *Maal og Minne, 1-2*, 89-107.

Takahashi, S. (1996). Pragmatic transferability. *Studies in Second Language Acquisition, 18*, 189-223.

Takahashi, S. (2001). The role of input enhancement in developing pragmatic competence. In K. Rose & G. Kasper (Eds.), *Pragmatics in language teaching* (pp.171-199). Cambridge: Cambridge University Press.

Takahashi, T., & Beebe, L. (1987). The development of pragmatic competence by Japanese learners of English. *JALT Journal, 8*, 131-155.

Takahashi, S., & DuFon, P. (1989). *Cross-linguistic influence in indirectness: The case of English directives performed by native Japanese speakers*. Unpublished manuscript, University of Hawai'i at Manoa, Honolulu. (ERIC Document Reproduction Service No. ED 370 439)

Trosborg, A. (1987). Apology strategies in natives/nonnatives. *Journal of Pragmatics, 11*, 147-167.

Trosborg, A. (1995). *Interlanguage pragmatics: Requests, complaints, and apologies*. Berlin: Mouton de Gruyter.

van Ek, J. A. (1976). *The threshold level for modern language learning in schools*. London: Longman.

浅野博他．(1997). *NEW HORIZON English Course*. 東京：東京書籍．
小篠敏明編．(1983).『英語教育学モノグラフ・シリーズ　英語の誤答分析』東京：大修館書店．
深澤清治．(1997).「日本人英語学習者の Pragmatic Competence 研究の応用―英語教科書に見られる refusal の分析を中心に―」『中国地区英語教育学会紀要』No. 27, pp. 287-292.
深澤清治．(2000).「Pragmatic sensitivity を育てる教材開発への示唆的研究」『中国地区英語教育学会紀要』No. 30, pp. 229-234.
文部省．(1998).『中学校学習指導要領』東京：大蔵省印刷局．

Appendix A

　このテストは、機能のつながりかたの難易度を調査し、会話の発展のしかたや会話構造を学ぶための教材を作成するための参考とするためのものです。このテストの結果は、すべて統計的に処理をするので、みなさんの個々人の成績には一切関係ありません。また、問題を解く時間的な制限はありませんので、すべての問題をやりとげてください。
　なお、問題用紙、解答用紙どちらも集めますし、テスト後、確かめなければならない事柄が生じたときの問い合わせのために必要ですので、必ず、<u>学校名、学年、組、番号、性別、氏名を記入</u>してから、始めてください。

《問題用紙》

学校名（　　）中学校	学年（　　）年	組（　　）組	番号（　　）番
性別（男／女）	氏名		

　次の機能に対して、つながりかたが自然であると思う機能には○を、つながりかたが不自然であると思う機能には×を、解答欄に記入してください。　例えば、1～7の7つの選択肢のうち、3、6、7はともにつながりかたが自然であるが1、2、4、5はともにつながりかたが不自然であると思う場合には、解答用紙の記入例のように記入することになります。
　なお、各機能において（　　）が併記されているものは、その機能が（　　）内の機能も含むという意味です。(例えば、Saying you are curious (Asking for information) という場合は、「好奇心をそそられると述べること」という機能と「事実情報を求めること」という機能とが重複しているということを表しています。)また、2つの機能が「—」で結ばれているものは、それらの機能がつながって生じるという意味です。(例えば、Greeting someone — Inviting someone という場合は、「あいさつをすること」という機能のあとに「だれかを誘うこと」という機能が続いて観察されるということを表しています。)
　それでは、以下の (A) から (S) までのすべての問題について、解答用紙の記入例にしたがい解答をしてください。

(A) Saying you are pessimistic (Saying you are worried or afraid)
　　「悲観的であることを表現すること（懸念・心配・恐れを表現すること）」

1. Asking for reasons (Trying to change someone's opinion (including arguing back))
「理由をたずねること（ある人の意見を変えようと試みること（反論することを含む））」
2. Saying you are bored (Being sarcastic about something)
「うんざりしていることを表現すること（あることについて皮肉を言うこと）」

(B) Saying you approve
「～を是認する、～に賛成する、と述べること」
1. Saying you are pleased
「喜びを表現すること」
2. Saying you have reached agreement
「意見が一致した、と述べること」

(C) Saying you do not approve
「～を是認しない、～に賛成しない、賛成しかねる、と述べること」
1. Saying you are worried or afraid (Talking about what might happen)
「懸念・心配・恐れを表現すること。(何が起こりうるかについて話すこと)」
2. Complimenting
「相手をほめること」

(D) Saying you are interested
「興味があることを表現すること」
1. Agreeing
「同意すること」
2. Asking for information
「事実情報を求めること」

(E) Demeaning oneself
「自分自身を卑下すること」
1. Agreeing
「同意すること」
2. Calming or reassuring someone
「だれかを落ち着かせる　あるいは安心させること」

(F) Expressing surprise
「驚きを表現すること」
1. Identifying/Reporting
「特定の人物・事物・場所・日時を見極めること／事実関係を報告したり、描写すること」

2. Saying you are curious (Asking for information)
「好奇心をそそられると述べること。(事実情報を求めること)」
3. Saying something is correct
「ある事柄が正しいと述べること」
(G) Saying you are excited
「興奮していることを表現すること」
1. Reporting
「事実情報を報告したり、描写すること」
2. Saying you are disappointed
「失望感、絶望感を表現すること」
3. Saying you are excited
「興奮していることを表現すること」
(H) Making an excuse (including explaining the details)
「言い訳をすること (ことの詳細を説明することを含む)」
1. Showing you are listening
「聞いていることを示すこと。あいづちをうつなど」
2. Finding out about meaning
「意味を見いだすこと」
3. Saying you understand
「わかった、と述べること」
(I) Being sarcastic about something
「ある事柄について皮肉を言うこと」
1. Greeting someone — Inviting someone
「あいさつをすること」—「だれかを誘うこと」
2. Attracting someone's attention — Telling someone to do something
「だれかの注意をひくこと」—「だれかにあることをするように言うこと」
3. Denying something
「ある事柄を否定すること」
(J) Saying you are displeased or angry
「不快あるいは怒りを表現すること」
1. Saying you are worried or afraid (Talking about what might happen)
「懸念・心配・恐れを表現すること。(何が起こりうるかについて話すこと)」
2. Saying sorry.
「謝罪すること」

3. Saying you approve
「～を是認する、～に賛成する、と述べること」
4. Showing you are listening
「聞いていることを示すこと。あいづちをうつなど」

(K) Calming or reassuring someone
「だれかを落ち着かせる　あるいは安心させること」
1. Asking if someone is sure about something
「あることについて確信があるかどうかたずねること」
2. Calling someone's name
「だれかを求めて叫ぶこと」
3. Turning something into joke
「ある事柄を冗談にすること、茶化すこと」
4. Saying you know about something
「ある事柄を知っていると述べること」

(L) Giving reasons
「理由を述べること」
1. Saying you understand
「わかった、と述べること」
2. Agreeing
「同意すること」
3. Reporting
「事実情報を報告したり、描写すること」
4. Showing you are listening
「聞いていることを示すこと。あいづちをうつなど」

(M) Blaming someone
「だれかをとがめること。非難すること」
1. Saying sorry
「謝罪すること」
2. Calming or reassuring someone
「だれかを落ち着かせる　あるいは安心させること」
3. Giving yourself time to think ― Saying someone must not do something
「考慮中の表現」―「してはいけない、と述べること」
4. Giving yourself time to think ― Making an excuse (including explaining the details)
「考慮中の表現」―「言い訳をすること（ことの詳細を説明することを含む）」

(N) Saying you are curious (Asking for information)
「好奇心をそそられると述べること（事実情報を求めること）」
　1. Identifying/Reporting
　　「特定の人物・事物・場所・日時を見極めること／事実情報を報告したり描写すること」
　2. Warning someone
　　「何かに気をつけるよう警告したり、注意を喚起すること」
　3. Saying you do not know
　　「知らないと述べること」
　4. Saying what you think is possible or probable
　　「～と考えられると表現すること」
　5. Asking back
　　「問い返すこと」
(O) Asking about likes
「相手の好みについてたずねること」
　1. Expressing likes
　　「好みを表現すること」
　2. Expressing dislikes
　　「嫌悪を表現すること」
　3. Expressing likes (Acknowledging something for the present)
　　「好みを表現すること（さしあたって、ある事柄を認めること）」
　4. Suggesting
　　「～してはどうか、と提案すること」
　5. Saying you remember ― Saying what you prefer
　　「覚えていると述べること」―「選択的に好みを表現すること。～の方が～よりも好きであると述べること」
(P) Giving your opinion
「自分の意見を述べること」
　1. Saying you partly agree (Comparing)
　　「部分的に同意すること（あることと比較すること）」
　2. Saying something is correct
　　「ある事柄が正しいと述べること」
　3. Agreeing
　　「同意すること」
　4. Trying to change someone's opinion (including arguing back)
　　「ある人の意見を変えようと試みること（反論することを含む）」

    5. Turning something into a joke
        「ある事柄を冗談にすること、茶化すこと」
(Q) Saying how you feel after something has happened
    「何かが起こった後、どのように感じているかを述べること」
    1. Agreeing
        「同意すること」
    2. Asking for information
        「事実情報を求めること」
    3. Reporting
        「事実情報を報告したり、描写すること」
    4. Saying you are pleased
        「喜びを表現すること」
    5. Showing you are listening
        「聞いていることを示すこと。あいづちをうつなど」
(R) Asking for reasons
    「理由をたずねること」
    1. Saying you do not know
        「知らないと述べること」
    2. Giving reasons
        「理由を述べること」
    3. Giving reasons (Covering up a fact)
        「理由を述べること（事実をかくすこと）」
    4. Inviting someone
        「だれかを誘うこと」
    5. Justifying oneself
        「自分を正当化すること」
    6. Asking back
        「問い返すこと」
(S) Trying to change someone's opinion (including arguing back)
    「ある人の意見を変えようと試みること（反論することを含む）」
    1. Calming or reassuring someone
        「だれかを落ち着かせる　あるいは安心させること」
    2. Saying you partly agree
        「部分的に同意すること」

3. Trying to change someone's opinion (including arguing back) (Talking about what might happen)
「ある人の意見を変えようと試みること（反論することを含む）。(何が起こりうるかについて話すこと)」
4. Justifying oneself
「自分自身を正当化すること」
5. Making an excuse (including explaining the details)
「言い訳をすること（ことの詳細を説明することを含む）」
6. Saying you intend to do something
「何かをする意志・意向のあるということを述べること」
7. Despising something (someone)
「ある事柄（ある人）を軽蔑・侮蔑すること」

問題用紙、解答用紙どちらも集めますし、テスト後、確かめなければならない事柄が生じたときの問い合わせのために必要ですので、必ず、<u>学校名、学年、組、番号、性別、氏名を記入</u>してから始めてください。

《解答用紙》

学校名（　　）中学校	学年（　　）年	組（　　）組	番号（　　）番
性別（男／女）	氏名		

※　つながりかたが自然であると思う機能には〇を記入
　　つながりかたが不自然であると思う機能には×を記入

記入例	1. ×	2. ×	3. 〇	4. ×	5. ×	6. 〇	7. 〇
(A)	1.	2.					
(B)	1.	2.					
(C)	1.	2.					
(D)	1.	2.					
(E)	1.	2.					
(F)	1.	2.	3.				
(G)	1.	2.	3.				
(H)	1.	2.	3.				
(I)	1.	2.	3.				
(J)	1.	2.	3.	4.			
(K)	1.	2.	3.	4.			
(L)	1.	2.	3.	4.			
(M)	1.	2.	3.	4.			
(N)	1.	2.	3.	4.	5.		
(O)	1.	2.	3.	4.	5.		
(P)	1.	2.	3.	4.	5.		
(Q)	1.	2.	3.	4.	5.		
(R)	1.	2.	3.	4.	5.	6.	
(S)	1.	2.	3.	4.	5.	6.	7.

Appendix B

学校名（　　　　　　　　）（　）年（　）組（　）番　（男　女）
　　　　　　　　　氏名（　　　　　　　　　　）

次の（　）に入れるのに最も適切なものを1，2，3，4の中から一つ選び、（　）の中にその番号を入れなさい。

1. My father wanted to be a police officer (　　) he was a child.
   1 that　　2 how　　3 so　　4 when
2. My sister is working at a flower shop. She must (　　) all the names of the flowers there.
   1 remember　　2 remembered　　3 to remember　　4 remembering
3. A: Are you going to (　　) the new movie tonight, Amy?
   B: Yes. Do you want to come with me?
   1 see　　2 saw　　3 seeing　　4 sees
4. There (　　) a lot of oranges on the trees now.
   1 be　　2 is　　3 are　　4 was
5. A: What did you do yesterday, Bill?
   B: I (　　) English and math.
   1 studied　　2 study　　3 studies　　4 studying
6. I'm not a good tennis player but I like (　　) tennis games.
   1 watched　　2 watch　　3 watches　　4 watching
7. This is (　　) popular computer game in Japan now.
   1 the most　　2 more　　3 much　　4 many
8. George (　　) his friends in the park yesterday.
   1 sees　　2 will see　　3 saw　　4 seen
9. A: You (　　) happy, Lucy.
   B: Yes, I am. I got a cute dog for my birthday.
   1 know　　2 look　　3 show　　4 stand
10. This video game is (　　) popular than that one.
    1 much　　2 many　　3 most　　4 more
11. A: Hi, Anne. Is this your textbook?
    B: Yes, it's (　　). Thank you.
    1 I　　2 my　　3 me　　4 mine

12. A: Mom, can I go to Kate's house? I left my homework there.
    B: OK, but it'll be dark soon. (　　) careful.
    1 Being　　2 Be　　3 Is　　4 Are
13. A: Did you (　　) to see a movie on Saturday?
    B: Yes, I did.
    1 go　　2 goes　　3 going　　4 to go
14. This skirt is (　　) than that one.
    1 cheap　　2 cheaper　　3 cheapest　　4 the cheapest
15. A: (　　) do you like better, coffee or tea?
    B: I like coffee.
    1 Who　　2 When　　3 Which　　4 Where
16. A: (　　) your homework. You can play with your friends later.
    B: OK, Mom.
    1 Finish　　2 Finishing　　3 Finished　　4 To finish
17. (　　) play your radio here, Jack. Your little brother is sleeping in the next room.
    1 Didn't　　2 Don't　　3 Does　　4 Did
18. A: Do you know the way to the station?
    B: Sure. I'll (　　) you the way.
    1 show　　2 shows　　3 showed　　4 showing
19. A: Do you want something (　　)?
    B: No, thanks. I'm not hungry.
    1 eat　　2 eats　　3 ate　　4 to eat
20. A: (　　) did you go home so early yesterday, Ann?
    B: Because we had a birthday party for my grandmother.
    1 When　　2 Why　　3 What　　4 Where
21. Mr. Harada went to Kenya (　　) pictures of African animals.
    1 takes　　2 took　　3 taken　　4 to take
22. Mark believes (　　) learning a foreign language will help him get a job in the future.
    1 what　　2 which　　3 when　　4 that
23. I don't know (　　) Central Park is.
    1 who　　2 when　　3 where　　4 whose
24. A: How long has your grandfather (　　) in Tokushima?
    B: All his life.
    1 lived　　2 lives　　3 living　　4 to live
25. Mrs. Yamada showed me many beautiful pictures (　　) at her wedding.
    1 taken　　2 taking　　3 takes　　4 took

26. A: Do you know the man (　) with Ms. Johnson over there?
　　B: No, I don't know him.
　　1 speak　　2 speaking　　3 spoke　　4 spoken
27. A: Have you (　) to the new library, Yoko?
　　B: Yes. It has a lot of English books.
　　1 be　　2 been　　3 are　　4 were
28. My sister is learning (　) to drive a car. She hopes to get her driver's license next month.
　　1 that　　2 whose　　3 what　　4 how
29. Mr. Smith showed me the pictures (　) he took during his stay in Hawaii.
　　1 how　　2 who　　3 which　　4 whose
30. A: You bought a new camera yesterday, (　) you?
　　B: Yes. It's a digital one.
　　1 didn't　　2 could　　3 haven't　　4 were
31. Many tourists come to Kyoto because there are a lot of places (　)
　　1 visit　　2 visited　　3 to visit　　4 visiting
32. Everybody, (　) quiet, please. I have good news.
　　1 be　　2 is　　3 are　　4 being
33. I don't know (　) Mary is coming back home tonight.
　　1 who　　2 whom　　3 what　　4 when
34. My family went shopping at a large supermarket (　) had many things on sale.
　　1 who　　2 what　　3 whose　　4 which
35. Mr. Arnold gave me two books (　) by his son.
　　1 write　　2 written　　3 to write　　4 wrote
36. My little brother always asks me (　) a story to him before he goes to sleep.
　　1 to read　　2 to be read　　3 reading　　4 for reading
37. Alice (　) many friends to her birthday party yesterday.
　　1 invited　　2 invites　　3 was invited　　4 inviting
38. It takes more than six hours (　) to Osaka by car from here.
　　1 gets　　2 got　　3 get　　4 to get
39. A: Have a nice trip. I hope you enjoy (　) Chicago.
　　B: Thanks.
　　1 visit　　2 to visit　　3 visiting　　4 visited
40. A: I have a really bad cold.
　　B: I think you (　) go and see a doctor.
　　1 had　　2 did　　3 should　　4 would

41. A: How was the movie last night?
    B: Very ( ). I really enjoyed it. You should see it!
    1 excite   2 excites   3 excited   4 exciting
42. Sandra tried to buy some bananas from the supermarket, but they didn't have ( ) left.
    1 any   2 little   3 few   4 some
43. A: These paintings are really beautiful. Where did you get them?
    B: They ( ) to me by a friend of mine.
    1 gave   2 were giving   3 were given   4 will give
44. A: Amy, you'd better ( ) now if you want to catch the last train.
    B: OK. See you tomorrow.
    1 leave   2 leaving   3 to leave   4 to be left
45. Louise has two pet dogs. One is white, and ( ) is brown. She gives them food every day.
    1 the other   2 others   3 other   4 another
46. The students could not help ( ) at the performance of our drama club.
    1 laugh   2 laughing   3 is laughing   4 laughed
47. Takeshi and Hiroko ( ) at Frank's house since last weekend. They will go back to Japan tomorrow.
    1 will be staying   2 stay   3 have been staying   4 stayed
48. If I had arrived at the festival earlier, I could ( ) the opening show.
    1 to watch   2 watched   3 have watched   4 had watched
49. A: Do you mind ( ) I turn on the radio?
    B: Not at all.
    1 what   2 if   3 or   4 which
50. A: Isn't this the hamburger shop ( ) you worked during high school?
    B: Yes. I worked here for two years.
    1 what   2 how   3 when   4 where
51. We have to be at the station by 7:30; ( ) we will miss the train and be late for the party.
    1 though   2 otherwise   3 unless   4 if
52. A: Look! The window's open.
    B: That's strange. I remember ( ) it last night.
    1 closed   2 closing   3 to close   4 to have closed
53. I can't find my red umbrella. I must ( ) it in the restaurant last night.
    1 be leaving   2 leave   3 have left   4 be left

54. Tom gave Jennifer (　) all of the grapes, and only ate a few himself.
   1 almost　　2 much　　3 only　　4 best
55. A: Have you met Mr. Mumford before?
   B: Yes, but it was several years ago, so I can't remember exactly (　) I met him.
   1 what　　2 which　　3 who　　4 where
56. A: I'd like to buy this jacket, but there's a small hole in it. Do you have (　) one?
   B: I'll just have a look.
   1 other　　2 another　　3 each other　　4 all the other
57. A: When is the soccer match?
   B: It's scheduled (　) next Saturday.
   1 held　　2 to hold　　3 to be held　　4 being held
58. I don't know (　) this artist is famous or not, but his paintings are wonderful.
   1 which　　2 where　　3 whether　　4 unless
59. Emily has a number of guitars. Two are classical guitars, and (　) are electric.
   1 another one　　2 another　　3 the others　　4 the ones
60. The doctor suggested that I (　) this medicine twice a day.
   1 take　　2 to take　　3 taking　　4 be taken

Appendix C

学校名（　　　　）（　）年（　）組（　）番（男　女）氏名（　　　　　）

次の①〜⑮の問題は、AさんからBさんへの英語の会話のつながりかたについての問題です。
下の例題にならって、それぞれの問題の指示にしたがって、（　　）の中に1，2，3を書き入れなさい。

・例題、③、⑦、⑩、⑪、⑬、⑮のアンダーラインがひいてある語は、その語を強く発音することを意味します。
・場面、AさんとBさんの関係、ストーリー、せりふのつながりかたが問題ごとに示してありますので、必ずそれらをよく読んで確かめたうえで指示にしたがって答えなさい。

例題
場面：教室
AさんとBさんの関係：先生→人形（目上の人→目下の人）
ストーリー：先生が、幼稚園児達に新しい単語を紹介するために人形を使って会話をしてみせています。
せりふのつながりかた：（先生）あることについて知っているかどうかたずねる
　　　　　　　　　　　→（人形）知っているかどうかを言う

[指示]次の人形のせりふの中で、知っていることを一番明確に述べているせりふには1、知っていることを二番目に明確に述べているせりふには2、知っていることをあまり明確に述べていないせりふには3を（　　）に書き入れなさい

A（先生）：	Do you know of any words that end in the same sound?		of...　…に関して、…について
B（人形）：	ア　I'll <u>try</u>.	（ 3 ）	words　語
	イ　Yes.	（ 2 ）	...that 〜　〜である…
	ウ　Yes, I know many words that end in the same sound.	（ 1 ）	end in ...　…で終わる I'll ＝ I will try...　…を試してみる

ウのせりふは、たくさんの単語の知識を持っていてそれを答えることができることを明確に示しています。イのせりふは、いくらかの単語を知っていることは聞き手（先生）に伝えてはいますが、それが少しの知識なのか多くの

知識なのかはこのせりふからはわかりません。アのせりふは、先生の問いに答えようという努力は示していますが、話し手の知識があるかないかは少しも示していません。したがって、この場面では、知っていることを一番明確に述べているせりふはウ、知っていることを二番目に明確に述べているせりふはイ、知っていることをあまり明確に述べていないせりふはアとなるので、ウに（1）、イに（2）、アに（3）と書き入れることになります。

それでは、この例題にならって、次の①から⑮の問題を解いてください。

① 場面：教室
　　AさんとBさんの関係：人形→先生（目下の人→目上の人）
　　ストーリー：先生が、幼稚園児達にある表現を教えるために、人形を使って会話をしてみせています。
　　せりふのつながりかた：（人形）助けを求める→（先生）助けを申し出る
[指示]次の先生のせりふの中で、積極的にすぐに助けを申し出ている一番適切なせりふには1、二番目に積極的に助けを申し出ているせりふには2、それほど適切に助けを申し出てはいないせりふには3を（　）に書き入れなさい。

A（人形）：	Will you help me?	
B（先生）：	ア　How can I help you?	（　）
	イ　I'll do it for you.	（　）
	ウ　We'll be happy to help.	（　）

Will you ...? …してくれませんか
I'll ＝ I will
We'll ＝ We will

② 場面：教室
　　AさんとBさんの関係：先生→人形（目上の人→目下の人）
　　ストーリー：先生が、幼稚園児達にある表現を教えるために、人形を使って会話をしてみせています。
　　せりふのつながりかた：（先生）好き・嫌いについてたずねる→（人形）好みを表現する
[指示]次の人形のせりふの中で、一番強く好みを表現している最も適切なせりふには1、二番目に強く好みを表現しているせりふには2、あまり強く好みを表現していないせりふには3を（　）に書き入れなさい。

A（先生）：	What is your favorite kind of day?	
B（人形）：	ア　I like rainy spring days.	（　）
	イ　I love days when the sun is out, the sky is blue, and there are no clouds.	（　）
	ウ　Warm days are OK.	（　）

kind　種類
...when ～　～である（ときの）…
out　出て
cloud　雲

③　場面：教室
　　Aさんとbさんの関係：人形→先生（目下の人→目上の人）
　　ストーリー：先生が、幼稚園児達にある表現を教えるために、人形を使って会話をしてみせています。
　　せりふのつながりかた：（人形）意見が同じか同じでないかについてたずねる→（先生）自信をもった断言

[指示]次の先生のせりふの中で、一番自信を持って断言しているせりふには1、二番目に自信を持って断言しているせりふには2、自信を持って断言する気持ちが一番弱いせりふには3を（　）に書き入れなさい。

A（人形）:	Do you think the children have favorite kinds of days?	kind　種類
B（先生）:	ア　I guess so.　　　　　　　　　　　（　）	
	イ　I'm sure they do.　　　　　　　　（　）	
	ウ　I think they do.　　　　　　　　　（　）	

④　場面：教室
　　AさんとBさんの関係：人形→先生（目下の人→目上の人）
　　ストーリー：先生が、幼稚園児達にある表現を教えるために、人形を使って会話をしてみせています。
　　せりふのつながりかた：（人形）不満を言う→（先生）元気づける

[指示]次の先生のせりふの中で、一番はっきりと相手を元気づけていて人形のせりふから自然につながるせりふには1、人形のせりふから自然につながるがあまりはっきりと相手を元気づけていないせりふには2、人形のせりふからそれほど自然にはつながっていないせりふには3を（　）に書き入れなさい。

A（人形）:	I don't have very many books.	very　［否定文で］
	I don't have the money to buy them.	あまり（…でない）
B（先生）:	ア　Maybe you don't need money.　　（　）	maybe　たぶん、ことによると
	イ　There is another way you can enjoy books.　（　）	way　方法
	ウ　You don't have to buy books to enjoy them.　（　）	

⑤　場面：教室
　　AさんとBさんの関係：先生→人形（目上の人→目下の人）
　　ストーリー：先生が、幼稚園児達にある表現を教えるために、人形を使って会話をしてみせています。

せりふのつながりかた：(先生)報告する→(人形)興味を表現する

[指示]次の人形のせりふの中で、興味を一番強く表している最も適切なせりふには1、どちらかといえば興味を表しているせりふには2、あまり興味を表していないせりふには3を（　）に書き入れなさい。

A（先生）：	There is a place where you can borrow books.		...where ～　～である
B（人形）：	ア　I see.	（　）	（ところの）…
	イ　That's nice.	（　）	～する（ところの）…
	ウ　There is?	（　）	borrow …を借りる

⑥　場面：学校内の部屋

　　AさんとBさんの関係：生徒→生徒（友達関係、同等の関係）

　　ストーリー：一人の生徒が美術の授業の準備のためにテーブルを動かしています。彼は、テーブルが重いので助けを求めます。

　　せりふのつながりかた：(生徒A)助けを求める→(生徒B)助けを申し出る

[指示]次の生徒Bのせりふの中で、積極的に助けを申し出ている一番適切なせりふには1、二番目に積極的に助けを申し出ているせりふには2、助けを申し出る気持ちはあまり強く表現していないせりふには3を（　）に書き入れなさい。

A（生徒）：	Could you push this table for me?		push　押す
B（生徒）：	ア　Sure. I'll do it now.	（　）	I'll = I will
	イ　Where do you want to push it to?	（　）	moment　ちょっとの間
	ウ　Yes, but wait a moment, please.	（　）	

⑦　場面：会社（オフィス）

　　AさんとBさんの関係：同僚（同等の関係）

　　ストーリー：彼らはオフィスにいて、昼食に何を食べようかを決めているところです。

　　せりふのつながりかた：(職員A)好き・嫌いについてたずねる→(職員B)好みを表現する

[指示]次の職員Bのせりふの中で、一番適切に好みを表していて職員Aのせりふから自然につながるせりふには1、好みの表し方やせりふのつながりかたが二番目に適切なせりふには2、あまり適切に好みを表現しているとはいえず、それほど自然につながらないせりふには3を（　）に書き入れなさい。

A（職員）：	Do you like pizza?		pizza ピザパイ
B（職員）：	ア Cheese pizza is delicious.	（ ）	cheese チーズ
	イ I eat pizza <u>sometimes</u>.	（ ）	delicious おいしい
	ウ Pizza is my favorite Italian food.	（ ）	Italian イタリアの

⑧　場面：オフィス
　　AさんとBさんの関係：同僚（同等の関係）
　　ストーリー：同僚／教職員が現在のカリキュラム（教育課程）について討
　　　　　　　　論しています。彼らは、変えていくことを提案しています。
　　せりふのつながりかた：（教職員A）意見が同じか同じでないかについて
　　　　　　　　　　　　　たずねる→（教職員B）自信を持った断言
[指示]次の教職員Bのせりふの中で、一番自信を持って断言しているせりふ
　　　には1、二番目に自信を持って断言しているせりふには2、自信を持っ
　　　て断言する気持ちが一番弱いせりふには3を（　　）に書き入れなさい。

A（教職員）：	Do you think Japanese students should study English more?		Japanese 日本の
B（教職員）：	ア I think they should study more.	（ ）	more もっと
	イ I would like to see them study.	（ ）	would like to see...
	ウ They definitely should study more.	（ ）	…してほしい
			definitely 確かに

⑨　場面：いなかの道路上。家から2時間離れている。
　　AさんとBさんの関係：親→10代の息子（目上の人→目下の人）
　　ストーリー：家から2時間離れたところでガソリンが少なくなってきまし
　　　　　　　　た。父親（運転手）がこのことに気がついて、案じています。
　　　　　　　　息子は元気づけようとしています。
　　せりふのつながりかた：（父親）不満を言う→（10代の息子）元気づける
[指示]次の10代の息子のせりふの中で、一番適切に相手を元気づけているこ
　　　とになるせりふには1、元気づける意味のせりふとしては二番目に適切なせ
　　　りふには2、あまり相手を元気づけていないせりふには3を（　　）に書
　　　き入れなさい。

A（父親）：	Oh, no. We are far from home and I am almost out of gasoline.		out of gasoline ガソリンが切れて
B（10代の息子）：	ア Don't worry. There is a gas station just ahead.	（ ）	gas station ガソリンスタンド
	イ Let's keep going.	（ ）	ahead 前方に
	ウ Let's try to find a gas station on the map.	（ ）	map 地図

⑩　場面：いなかの道路上。家から２時間離れている。
　　Ａさんと B さんの関係：10代の息子→親（目下の人→目上の人）
　　ストーリー：（⑨の問題の）息子が、今、父親に、すぐそばにガソリンスタンドがあると伝えます。
　　せりふのつながりかた：（10代の息子）報告する→（父親）興味を表現する

[指示]次の父親のせりふの中で、興味を一番強く表している最も適切なせりふには１、どちらかといえば興味を表しているせりふには２、あまり興味を表していないせりふには３を（　　）に書き入れなさい。

A（10代の息子）：	There is a gas station just ahead.		gas station　ガソリンスタンド
B（父親）：	ア　Oh, great! There is a gas station just ahead.	（　）	ahead　前方に
	イ　Oh, OK.	（　）	
	ウ　Yes? Is it on the left?	（　）	

⑪　場面：家
　　Ａさんと B さんの関係：上役、上司→従業員（目上の人→目下の人）
　　ストーリー：上司がその日遅れて駅に着きます。上司が部下に特定の時刻に迎えにきてくれるように頼みます。
　　せりふのつながりかた：（上役／上司）助けを求める→（従業員）助けを申し出る

[指示]次の従業員のせりふの中で、確実な助けを一番強く申し出ているせりふには１、助けを申し出ているがその気持ちがそれほど明確ではないせりふには２、助けを申し出る気持ちが最も弱くこの場面では適切でないせりふには３を（　　）に書き入れなさい。

A（上役／上司）：	Will you pick me up at 3 o'clock at the train station?		Will you...?　…してくれませんか
B（従業員）：	ア　OK. But let me check my schedule first.	（　）	pick...up　…を車に乗せる（迎えに行く）
	イ　Sure. I'll see you at three.	（　）	let ... ～　…に～させる
	ウ　Yes, I should be there by three.	（　）	check　チェックする
			schedule　予定
			should　おそらく（きっと）…であろう

⑫　場面：教室
　　Aさんとbさんの関係：生徒→先生（目下の人→目上の人）
　　ストーリー：生徒達が先生と自由に話をしています。彼らは学校について
　　　　　　　　たくさんの質問をしています。
　　せりふのつながりかた：（生徒）好き・嫌いについてたずねる→（先生）
　　　　　　　　　　　　　好みを表現する
[指示]次の先生のせりふの中で、一番強く好みを表現している最も適切なせりふには1、二番目に好みを適切に表現しているせりふには2、あまり強く好みを表現していないせりふには3を（　　）に書き入れなさい。

A（生徒）:	What subject do you like the best?	
B（先生）:	ア　I have fun in English.	（　）
	イ　I love science.	（　）
	ウ　Math is OK.	（　）

⑬　場面：教室
　　AさんとBさんの関係：先生→生徒（目上の人→目下の人）
　　ストーリー：地理学の先生が、生徒のその日の授業の理解度を確かめるた
　　　　　　　　めにたずねています。
　　せりふのつながりかた：（先生）意見が同じか同じでないかについてたず
　　　　　　　　　　　　　ねる→（生徒）自信を持った断言
[指示]次の生徒のせりふの中で、一番自信を持って断言しているせりふには1、あまり自信を持って断言していないせりふには2、自信を持って断言する気持ちが一番弱いせりふには3を（　　）に書き入れなさい。

A（先生）:	Isn't Australia bigger than Canada?		Isn't ...? …でしょう？
B（生徒）:	ア　Australia seems smaller than the other country.	（　）	seem …のように見える、…らしい
	イ　Canada may be bigger.	（　）	may …かもしれない
	ウ　No, Australia <u>isn't</u> bigger than Canada.	（　）	

⑭　場面：教室
　　AさんとBさんの関係：生徒→生徒（友達関係、同等の関係）
　　ストーリー：日本の中学校の給食時間です。生徒達は机の上の食事を食べるためにちょうど座ったところです。ある生徒は、自分はあまりにも多くのごはんをつがれていると思っています。彼は不満をもらしますが、彼のクラスメートが彼を元気づけます。

せりふのつながりかた：（生徒A）不満を言う→（生徒B）元気づける
[指示] 次の生徒Bのせりふの中で、一番直接的にすぐに相手を元気づけている最も適切なせりふには1、二番目に適切に相手を元気づけているせりふには2、元気づける意味のせりふとしては生徒Aのせりふからそれほど自然につながっていないせりふには3を（　）に書き入れなさい。

A（生徒）：	Mr. Suenaga gave me too much rice for lunch.		what you don't want
B（生徒）：	ア　It's OK. Give me what you don't want.	（　）	あなたがほしくないもの
	イ　Let's talk to Mr. Suenaga.	（　）	
	ウ　You don't have to eat it.	（　）	

⑮　場面：大学の教室／オフィス／カウンターのある食堂
　　AさんとBさんの関係：大学の同級生（友達関係、同等の関係）
　　ストーリー：週末の後、2人のクラスメートが、自分達が週末何をしたかを話しています。1人が、買物にいって何を購入したかを述べます。
　　せりふのつながりかた：（大学生A）報告する→（大学生B）興味を表現する
[指示] 次の大学生Bのせりふの中で、興味を一番強く表している最も適切なせりふには1、どちらかといえば興味を表しているせりふには2、あまり興味を表していないせりふには3を（　）に書き入れなさい。

A（大学生）：	I have just bought a new SONY computer.		have just bought
B（大学生）：	ア　Is it nice?	（　）	ちょうど買ったところ
	イ　Oh, did you?	（　）	
	ウ　Oh, I have one, too.	（　）	

この問題を解いた全体的な感想、あるいは一つひとつの問題についての気づきを書いてください。

Appendix D

INFORMED CONSENT

The study in which you are being asked to participate in is designed to investigate the use of English by native speakers. This study is being conducted by Yoko Fujiwara under the supervision of Dr. Ozasa, Professor of the Graduate School of Education in Hiroshima University. This study has been approved by the Institutional Review Board, California State University, San Bernardino.

In this study you will be rating conversational responses according to how appropriate you think they are in the given situation. The questionnaire should take about 5 to 10 minutes to complete. All of your responses will be held in the strictest of confidence by the researchers. Your name will not be reported with your responses. All data will be reported in group form only. You may receive the group results of this study upon completion in the Winter Quarter of 2004 by e-mailing tozasa@hirohima-u.ac.jp

Your participation in this study is totally voluntary. You are free not to answer any questions and withdraw at any time during this study without penalty. When you have completed the questionnaire, you will receive a debriefing statement describing the study in more detail. In order to ensure the validity of the study, we ask that you not discuss this study with other students or participants.

If you have any questions or concerns about this study, please feel free to contact Dr. Ozasa at the Graduate School of Education in Hiroshima University at tozasa@hiroshima-u.ac.jp

By placing a check mark in the box below, I acknowledge that I have been informed of, and that I understand, the nature and purpose of this study, and I freely consent to participate. I also acknowledge that I am at least 18 years of age.

Place a check mark here ☐   **Today's date:** _____

Questionnaires

Gender (   )

> The following section of the questionnaire aims to find out your opinions about appropriateness in Junior High Schools in America.
> Here appropriateness means the extent to which a use of language matches the linguistic and sociolinguistic expectations and practices of native speakers of the English language. When formulating a sentence, a speaker needs to know that it is grammatical, and also that it is suitable (appropriate) for the particular situation.
> For example:
> > Give me a glass of water!
>
> is grammatical, but it would not be appropriate if the speaker wanted to be polite. A request such as:
> > May I have a glass of water, please?
>
> would be more appropriate.
> An utterance which is grammatically correct may still be deemed inappropriate, even when it is an honest expression of the speaker's thoughts, if it does not meet the sociolinguistic expectations of the situation. For example, if the utterance is too adult, dramatic, casual, rude, affected, formal, confident, flowery, a little too high level, not a typical response from a junior high school student, or overpolite for the particular setting (i.e., whether the person being spoken to is a student [junior high school student], peer, or teacher). If speech is too affected or overpolite, it may seem sarcastic.
> When answering each item, please rate each response on the scale of appropriateness, with (1) being inappropriate, and (3) being appropriate (as shown in the example below):
>
> > inappropriate ← 1 : 2 : 3 → appropriate

> (Ex.) Setting: A Japanese boy (Ken) is staying in America.
> > The day after he arrived at the Joneses' home.
>
> A(Mrs. Jones): Do you know how to make your bed?
> B(Ken) : a. No, I don't know how.   1 : 2 : ③
>   b. How should I know?   ① : 2 : 3
>
> Here, a. is appropriately polite because Ken (Low status) is answering to Mrs. Jones (High status). On the other hand, b. is inappropriate because Ken's words are casually impudent.

> The test will be presented in two mediums ——— 1) a questionnaire in

written form and 2) a tape-recording in audio form. Please read and listen carefully, paying attention to 1) the role relationships (the relative status of the speaker and the addressee —— in this test the relationships are people of high status talking to people of low status, people of low status talking to people of high status, and people in an equal relationship) and 2) the settings. Please rate the appropriateness of the addressee's responses, and circle the suitable number.

When rating the responses, please bear in mind the definition of inappropriateness provided, and apply it strictly. There are some responses in the test items which could be considered inappropriate in the vast majority of cases, but you can perhaps think of people or relationships which would make the response realistically appropriate. In these instances, please rate the response according to the appropriateness in the vast majority of cases —— this is more important in the test than the linguistic predilections of a tiny minority. It should be made clear that in these test items you must imagine the relationships between the teachers and students to be strictly formal, with the social expectations being rigidly observed (Please do not imagine a friendly bantering relationship between teachers and students, as this would distort the purpose of the test).

1. Setting: In a classroom. A discussion about technology.
   A (Teacher)   Do you think we need computers?
   B (Student)   a. Anyone can see that.   1 : 2 : 3
                 b. Yes, I think we do.   1 : 2 : 3

2. Setting: In a classroom. A discussion about technology.
   A (Student)   Do you think we need computers?
   B (Teacher)   a. That's obvious, isn't it?   1 : 2 : 3
                 b. Yes, they're very useful.   1 : 2 : 3

3. Setting: In a classroom. A discussion about technology.
              Two close friends are talking to each other.
   A (Student)   Do you think we need computers?
   B (Student)   a. Yeah, I think so.   1 : 2 : 3
                 b. Yes, I confirm it.   1 : 2 : 3

4. Setting: In a classroom. A discussion about summer holidays.
              Two close friends are talking to each other.

	A (Student)	I stayed in Canada last summer.	
	B (Student)	a. Did you do anything fun?	1 : 2 : 3
		b. What a splendid opportunity!	1 : 2 : 3

5. Setting: In a classroom. A discussion about summer holidays.
   A (Student) I stayed in Canada last summer.
   B (Teacher) a. Did you enjoy it?   1 : 2 : 3
                b. Really, I would give anything for a chance to go to Canada.
                                                                                   1 : 2 : 3

6. Setting: In a classroom. A discussion about summer holidays.
   A (Teacher) I stayed in Canada last summer.
   B (Student) a. What did you do there?   1 : 2 : 3
                b. Would you be so kind to tell me more?   1 : 2 : 3

7. Setting: During the class, the teacher tells the student.
   A (Teacher) I don't understand what you mean.
   B (Student) a. I'm sorry, let me try again.   1 : 2 : 3
                b. OK, I will use smaller words to explain.   1 : 2 : 3

8. Setting: During the class, the student calls out.
   A (Student) I don't understand what you mean.
   B (Teacher) a. Let me explain so that any child can understand.   1 : 2 : 3
                b. OK, let me explain in a different way.   1 : 2 : 3

9. Setting: During the class, one student speaks to another. They are close friends.
   A (Student) I don't understand what you mean.
   B (Student) a. Let me show you.   1 : 2 : 3
                b. Please allow me to explain again.   1 : 2 : 3

10. Setting: In a classroom. A teacher and students are preparing for the school festival. A teacher made a nice costume.
    A (Teacher) Do you like this costume?
    B (Student) a. It's great!   1 : 2 : 3
                 b. You might be able to say that.   1 : 2 : 3

11. Setting: In a classroom. A teacher and students are preparing for the school festival. A student made a nice costume.
    A (Student)   Do you like this costume?
    B (Teacher)   a. Wow, it is the most beautiful costume I have ever seen.
                              1 : 2 : 3
           b. Yes, I really like it.   1 : 2 : 3

12. Setting: In a classroom. A teacher and students are preparing for the school festival. A student made a nice costume. Two close friends are talking to each other.
    A (Student)   Do you like this costume?
    B (Student)   a. Yeah, you look nice in that costume. 1 : 2 : 3
           b. Yes, your costume is very nicely made. 1 : 2 : 3

13. Setting: In a classroom. The student requests help in answering a question.
    A (Student)   Will you help me?
    B (Teacher)   a. Certainly.   1 : 2 : 3
           b. Yeah, why not?   1 : 2 : 3

14. Setting: In a classroom. A student requests help in doing his homework.
    A (Student)   Will you help me?
    B (Student)   a. I would be glad to offer you assistance. 1 : 2 : 3
           b. Yeah, sure.   1 : 2 : 3

15. Setting: In a classroom. The teacher requests help in moving a table.
    A (Teacher)   Will you help me?
    B (Student)   a. Of course.   1 : 2 : 3
           b. Yes, if I have to.   1 : 2 : 3

16. Setting: In a classroom. A student is using a computer.
    A (Student)   Well, the computer isn't working well.
    B (Student)   a. Allow me to troubleshoot your machine and I will have it running perfectly. 1 : 2 : 3
           b. Don't worry. It's probably not so difficult to fix. 1 : 2 : 3

17. Setting: In a classroom. A student is using a computer.
    A (Student)   Excuse me. The computer isn't working well.
    B (Teacher)   a. Don't worry about it. I can fix it.   1 : 2 : 3
                  b. Everything is going to be all right. I can fix anything.
                                                                            1 : 2 : 3

18. Setting: In a classroom. A teacher is showing a teaching material to the students using a computer.
    A (Teacher)   Well, the computer isn't working well.
    B (Student)   a. Is there anything I can do?   1 : 2 : 3
                  b. Now, now, take it easy.   1 : 2 : 3

19. Setting: In a classroom. A discussion about winter sports.
    Two close friends are talking to each other.
    A (Student)   Do you like ice skating?
    B (Student)   a. Ice skating is what I most enjoy.   1 : 2 : 3
                  b. Yeah, it's fun.   1 : 2 : 3

20. Setting: In a classroom. A discussion about winter sports.
    A (Teacher)   Do you like ice skating?
    B (Student)   a. It is simply the most divine activity I have ever done.
                                                                            1 : 2 : 3
                  b. Yes, I really enjoy it.   1 : 2 : 3

21. Setting: In a classroom. A discussion about winter sports.
    A (Student)   Do you like ice skating?
    B (Teacher)   a. Yeah, ice skating is totally awesome. It's so cool, you know.
                                                                            1 : 2 : 3
                  b. Yes, I do.   1 : 2 : 3

22. Setting: In a parking area at school. A teacher asks a student to carry a very heavy bag for her.
    A (Teacher)   Will you help me?
    B (Student)   a. I guess I will if you can't do it yourself.   1 : 2 : 3
                  b. Sure, I can handle that.   1 : 2 : 3

23. Setting: In a faculty room. A student asks a music teacher to help him with writing music for his poem.
    A (Student)   Will you help me?
    B (Music teacher) a. I guess so.   1 : 2 : 3
                      b. Sure.   1 : 2 : 3

24. Setting: In a school. A student asks his friend to write music for his poem. They are close friends.
    A (Student) Will you help me?
    B (Student) a. I see no objection.   1 : 2 : 3
                b. No problem.   1 : 2 : 3

25. Setting: In a classroom. A discussion about the weekend.
    A (Teacher) I went to Disneyland this weekend.
    B (Student) a. How was it?   1 : 2 : 3
                b. Oh, tell me every little detail. I can't wait to hear. 1 : 2 : 3

26. Setting: In a classroom. A discussion about the weekend. Two close friends are talking to each other.
    A (Student) I went to Disneyland this weekend.
    B (Student) a. Indeed?   1 : 2 : 3
                b. Lucky you!   1 : 2 : 3

27. Setting: In a classroom. A discussion about the weekend.
    A (Student) I went to Disneyland this weekend.
    B (Teacher) a. Oh, what an enjoyable time you must have had!   1 : 2 : 3
                b. That sounds like fun.   1 : 2 : 3

28. Setting: In a classroom. A discussion about a new parking area plan.
    A (Teacher) Do you think we need another parking area?
    B (Student) a. Absolutely, and the sooner we get one the better.   1 : 2 : 3
                b. Yes, we certainly do.   1 : 2 : 3

29. Setting: In a classroom. A discussion about a new parking area plan. Two close friends are talking to each other.
    A (Student) Do you think we need another parking area?
    B (Student) a. That is my conviction.   1 : 2 : 3
                b. Yes, I do.   1 : 2 : 3

30. Setting: In a classroom. A discussion about a new parking area plan.
    A (Student)   Do you think we need another parking area?
    B (Teacher)   a. Yeah, we totally need a new parking area, man.   1 : 2 : 3
                   b. Yes, we do.   1 : 2 : 3

Please write any comments or thoughts you have about this test (or each test item) here.

DEBRIEFING STATEMENT

The Acquisition of English Function-chain:
With a Focus on Japanese EFL Learners

The study you have just completed was designed to help investigate the process of development of Japanese learners of English in acquiring pragmatic competence —— more specifically, to assess their development in recognizing appropriateness in spoken English. To do this it was necessary to get native English speakers to do the test, to act as a yardstick for assessing the responses from the Japanese participants.

Thank you for your participation. If you have any questions about the study, please feel free to contact Professor Ozasa at the Graduate School of Education in Hiroshima University at tozasa@hiroshima-u.ac.jp

If you would like to obtain a copy of the group results of this study, please contact Professor Ozasa at tozasa@hiroshima-u.ac.jp at the end of Winter Quarter of 2004.

Appendix E

（　　）年（　　）組（　　　）番（男　女）氏名（　　　　　　　　　　　　）

　次の1.から30.までの問題は、AさんからBさんへの会話のつながりかたについての問題です。Aさんのせりふに対してBさんの答え方がどれだけ適切であるかについてのみなさんの意見を求めています。これらの会話はアメリカの中学校での会話だと考えてください。
　ここでは、適切な答え方とは、どれだけその状況に合った言い方であるか、英語母語話者の方の習慣に合ったものであるかということです。あるせりふを発するとき、話し手は、それが文法的に正しい文かということと同時にその状況にふさわしい（適切な）言い方であるかということも知っている必要があります。
例えば：
　Give me a glass of water!
は文法的に正しい文です。しかし、もしその話し手がていねいに言いたいときにはそれは適切ではないでしょう。
　May I have a glass of water, please?
は、もっと適切な文だといえるでしょう。
　一方、不適切さとは、ここでは、そのせりふが文法的に正しくて、おそらく誠実な言い方ですらあるかもしれないけれども、その状況には適さないものをいいます。例えば、ある状況（つまり、生徒から先生に言うせりふか、友達どうしのせりふか、先生から生徒に言うせりふかという状況）にしては、あまりにも大人びた言い方、芝居がかったドラマティックな言い方、カジュアルすぎる言い方、無礼な言い方、気取りすぎた言い方、形式ばった堅苦しい言い方、自信がありすぎる言い方、美辞麗句を用いすぎた言い方、中学生にしてはハイレベルすぎて中学生はあまり使わない言い方、ていねいすぎる言い方は不適切であるといえます。あまりにも気取った言い方やていねいすぎる言い方は、ときには皮肉（いやみ）に聞こえるかもしれません。

　それぞれの問題に答える際には、下の（例）にならって、1から3までの3段階でBさんのせりふの適切さの程度を評価してください。

不適切← 1 : 2 : 3 →適切

> （例）場面：日本人の男の子、健がアメリカに滞在しています。
> 　　　　　彼がジョーンズ家に到着した翌日のこと。
> A（ジョーンズ夫人）： Do you know how to make your bed?
> B（健）　　　　　： a. No, I don't know how.　　　　　1 : 2 :③
> 　　　　　　　　　 b. How should I know?　　　　　　①: 2 : 3
> 　　　　　　　　　　　一体、どうして
> 　　ここでは、a. のせりふは目下の健が目上のジョーンズ夫人にていねいなことばで適切に答えているので3に○、b. のせりふは健のカジュアルな言い方が無礼で失礼なので1に○をつけます。

　みなさんは、この紙に書かれた問題を読むと同時にテープに吹き込まれた音声を聞いてBさんのせりふの適切さを判断していきます。注意深く英語を読み、CDから聞こえてくる英語を聞いて、AさんとBさんの人間関係や場面に注意して問題を解いてください。Bさんの答え方の適切さを評価して、不適切な言い方だと思えば1、どちらでもないと思えば2、適切な言い方だと思えば3に○をしてください。
　その際に、最初に示した不適切さの定義を心にとめて○をつけてください。このテストでは大部分の人は不適切だと考えるせりふは1に○をします。中にはそのような答え方をする人もいるだろうから、と考える必要はありません。不適切なせりふに関しては、少数の人の好みよりは、大部分の人はこのようには言わないだろうという基準で評価してください。また、先生と生徒の関係は厳密に伝統的なものであり、フレンドリーな冗談を言うような関係ではないと思ってください。

1. 場面：教室。科学技術についての話し合いの場面。
   A（先生）： Do you think we need computers?
   B（生徒）： a. Anyone can see that.　　　　　　　　1 : 2 : 3
   　　　　　　　　だれでも
   　　　　　　b. Yes, I think we do.　　　　　　　　　1 : 2 : 3

2. 場面：教室。科学技術についての話し合いの場面。
   A（生徒）： Do you think we need computers?
   B（先生）： a. That's obvious, isn't it?　　　　　　　1 : 2 : 3
   　　　　　　　　明らかな
   　　　　　　b. Yes, they're very useful.　　　　　　　1 : 2 : 3

3. 場面：教室。科学技術についての話し合いの場面。2人の親しい友達どうしで話している。
A（生徒）： Do you think we need computers?
B（生徒）： a. Yeah, I think so. 　　　　　　　　　　1 : 2 : 3
　　　　　　 b. Yes, I confirm it. 　　　　　　　　　　1 : 2 : 3
　　　　　　　　　確証する

4. 場面：教室。夏休みのことについて話している。2人の親しい友達どうしで話している。
A（生徒）： I stayed in Canada last summer.
B（生徒）： a. Did you do anything fun? 　　　　　　1 : 2 : 3
　　　　　　　　　　　　 何か
　　　　　　 b. What a splendid opportunity! 　　　　　1 : 2 : 3
　　　　　　　　　　 すばらしい　　機会

5. 場面：教室。夏休みのことについて話している。
A（生徒）： I stayed in Canada last summer.
B（先生）： a. Did you enjoy it? 　　　　　　　　　　 1 : 2 : 3
　　　　　　 b. Really, I would give anything for a chance to go to Canada.
　　　　　　　　　　　　　　　　 何でも　　　　機会、チャンス　　 1 : 2 : 3

6. 場面：教室。夏休みのことについて話している。
A（先生）： I stayed in Canada last summer.
B（生徒）： a. What did you do there? 　　　　　　　 1 : 2 : 3
　　　　　　 b. Would you be so kind to tell me more? 　 1 : 2 : 3
　　　　　　　　　　　　　　　　　　　　　 もっと

7. 場面：授業中、先生が生徒に言う。
A（先生）： I don't understand what you mean.
　　　　　　　　　　　　　　 あなたが意味すること
B（生徒）： a. I'm sorry, let me try again. 　　　　　　1 : 2 : 3
　　　　　　　　　　 …させて下さい
　　　　　　 b. OK, I will use smaller words to explain. 　1 : 2 : 3
　　　　　　　　　　　　　　　 ことば　　　 説明する

Appendices 127

8. 場面：授業中、生徒が叫ぶ。
A（生徒）： I don't understand what you mean.
B（先生）： a. Let me explain so that any child can understand.　1：2：3
　　　　　　　　…が〜できるように
　　　　　　b. OK, let me explain in a different way.　1：2：3

9. 場面：授業中、ある生徒がもう一人の生徒に話しかける。彼らは親しい友達である。
A（生徒）： I don't understand what you mean.
B（生徒）： a. Let me show you.　1：2：3
　　　　　　b. Please allow me to explain again.　1：2：3
　　　　　　　　…いたしましょう

10. 場面：教室。ある先生と生徒達が文化祭の準備をしている。先生はすてきな衣装を作った。
A（先生）： Do you like this costume?
B（生徒）： a. It's great!　1：2：3
　　　　　　b. You might be able to say that.　1：2：3
　　　　　　　　…かもしれない …できる

11. 場面：教室。ある先生と生徒達が文化祭の準備をしている。ある生徒がすてきな衣装を作った。
A（生徒）： Do you like this costume?
B（先生）： a. Wow, it is the most beautiful costume I have ever seen.
　　　　　　　　　　　　　　　　　　　　　　　　今まで見たうちで 1：2：3
　　　　　　b. Yes, I really like it.　1：2：3

12. 場面：教室。ある先生と生徒達が文化祭の準備をしている。ある生徒がすてきな衣装を作った。2人の親しい友達どうしで話している。
A（生徒）： Do you like this costume?
B（生徒）： a. Yeah, you look nice in that costume.　1：2：3
　　　　　　b. Yes, your costume is very nicely made.　1：2：3
　　　　　　　　　　　　　　りっぱに

13. 場面。教室。問題を解くのを手助けしてほしいと生徒がたのんでいる。
A（生徒）： Will you help me?
B（先生）： a. Certainly. 1 : 2 : 3
　　　　　　　　 もちろん
　　　　　　　b. Yeah, why not? 1 : 2 : 3
　　　　　　　　　　　　もちろん

14. 場面。教室。ある生徒が宿題を手伝ってほしいとたのんでいる。
A（生徒）： Will you help me?
B（生徒）： a. I would be glad to offer you assistance. 1 : 2 : 3
　　　　　　　　 喜んで…する 申し出る 助力
　　　　　　　b. Yeah, sure. 1 : 2 : 3

15. 場面。教室。先生が、テーブルを動かすのを手伝ってほしいとたのんでいる。
A（先生）： Will you help me?
B（生徒）： a. Of course. 1 : 2 : 3
　　　　　　　　 もちろん
　　　　　　　b. Yes, if I have to. 1 : 2 : 3

16. 場面。教室。ある生徒がコンピュータを使っている。
A（生徒）： Well, the computer isn't working well.
B（生徒）： a. Allow me to troubleshoot your machine and I will have it running
　　　　　　　　　　　　　 修理する　　　　　機械　　　　　…させる 動く
　　　　　　　perfectly. 1 : 2 : 3
　　　　　　　 完全に
　　　　　　　b. Don't worry. It's probably not so difficult to fix. 1 : 2 : 3
　　　　　　　　　　　　　　　　　　 たぶん　　　　　　　　　　 修理する

17. 場面：教室。ある生徒がコンピュータを使っている。
A（生徒）： Excuse me. The computer isn't working well.
B（先生）： a. Don't worry about it. I can fix it. 1 : 2 : 3
　　　　　　　b. Everything is going to be all right. I can fix anything. 1 : 2 : 3

18. 場面：教室。先生がコンピュータを使って生徒達に教材を見せている。
A（先生）： Well, the computer isn't working well.
B（生徒）： a. Is there <u>anything</u> I can do?　　　　　　　1 : 2 : 3
　　　　　　　　　　何か
　　　　　　b. <u>Now</u>, now, take it easy.　　　　　　　　　　1 : 2 : 3
　　　　　　　　さあ

19. 場面：教室。冬のスポーツについて話している。2人の親しい友達どうし
　　で話している。
A（生徒）： Do you like ice skating?
B（生徒）： a. Ice skating is <u>what</u> I most enjoy.　　　　　1 : 2 : 3
　　　　　　　　　　　　　　…であるもの
　　　　　　b. Yeah, it's fun.　　　　　　　　　　　　　　　1 : 2 : 3

20. 場面：教室。冬のスポーツについて話している。
A（先生）： Do you like ice skating?
B（生徒）： a. It is <u>simply</u> the most <u>divine</u> <u>activity</u> I have <u>ever done</u>. 1 : 2 : 3
　　　　　　　　　まったく、実に　　すばらしい　活動　　今までしたうちで
　　　　　　b. Yes, I really enjoy it.　　　　　　　　　　　1 : 2 : 3

21. 場面：教室。冬のスポーツについて話している。
A（生徒）： Do you like ice skating?
B（先生）： a. Yeah, ice skating is <u>totally</u> <u>awesome</u>. It's so cool, <u>you know</u>.
　　　　　　　　　　　　　　　すごく　すばらしい　　　　　…（です）ね
　　　　　　　　　　　　　　　　　　　　　　　　　　　　　1 : 2 : 3
　　　　　　b. Yes, I do.　　　　　　　　　　　　　　　　　1 : 2 : 3

22. 場面：学校の駐車場。先生がある生徒にとても重いかばんを運んでくれる
　　ようにたのむ。
A（先生）： Will you help me?
B（生徒）： a. I guess I will if you can't do it <u>yourself</u>.　　1 : 2 : 3
　　　　　　　　　　　　　　　　　　　　　　自分で
　　　　　　b. Sure, I can <u>handle</u> that.　　　　　　　　　　1 : 2 : 3
　　　　　　　　　　　　　取り扱う

23. 場面：職員室。ある生徒が、自分の詩に曲をつけるのを手伝ってくれるように音楽の先生にたのむ。
A（生徒）：　　　　　Will you help me?
B（音楽の先生）：　　a. I guess so.　　　　　　　　　　　　1：2：3
　　　　　　　　　　b. Sure.　　　　　　　　　　　　　　1：2：3

24. 場面：学校。ある生徒が、自分の詩に曲をつけるのを手伝ってくれるように友達にたのむ。彼らは親しい友達である。
A（生徒）：　　Will you help me?
B（生徒）：　　a. I see no objection.　　　　　　　　　　1：2：3
　　　　　　　　　　　反対、異議
　　　　　　　b. No problem.　　　　　　　　　　　　　1：2：3

25. 場面：教室。週末についての話をしている。
A（先生）：　　I went to Disneyland this weekend.
B（生徒）：　　a. How was it?　　　　　　　　　　　　　1：2：3
　　　　　　　b. Oh, tell me every little detail. I can't wait to hear.　1：2：3
　　　　　　　　　　　　　　　　　詳しい説明

26. 場面：教室。週末についての話をしている。2人の親しい友達どうしで話している。
A（生徒）：　　I went to Disneyland this weekend.
B（生徒）：　　a. Indeed?　　　　　　　　　　　　　　　1：2：3
　　　　　　　　　ほんとうに
　　　　　　　b. Lucky you!　　　　　　　　　　　　　　1：2：3

27. 場面：教室。週末についての話をしている。
A（生徒）：　　I went to Disneyland this weekend.
B（先生）：　　a. Oh, what an enjoyable time you must have had!　1：2：3
　　　　　　　　　　　　　　　楽しい　　　　　過ごしたにちがいない
　　　　　　　b. That sounds like fun.　　　　　　　　　　1：2：3

28. 場面：教室。新しい駐輪場の計画についての話をしている。
A（先生）：　　Do you think we need another parking area?
B（生徒）：　　a. Absolutely, and the sooner we get one the better.　1：2：3
　　　　　　　　　まったくその通り
　　　　　　　b. Yes, we certainly do.　　　　　　　　　　1：2：3

29. 場面：教室。新しい駐輪場の計画についての話をしている。2人の親しい
    友達どうしで話している。
A（生徒）：　　Do you think we need another parking area?
B（生徒）：　　a. That is my conviction.　　　　　　　　1 : 2 : 3
                      ‾‾‾‾‾‾‾‾‾‾
                      確信、信念
              b. Yes, I do.　　　　　　　　　　　　　　　1 : 2 : 3

30. 場面：教室。新しい駐輪場の計画についての話をしている。
A（生徒）：　　Do you think we need another parking area?
B（先生）：　　a. Yeah, we totally need a new parking area, man.　1 : 2 : 3
              b. Yes, we do.　　　　　　　　　　　　　　1 : 2 : 3

この問題を解いた全体的な感想、あるいは一つひとつの問題についての気づきを書いてください。

Name index

Bachman, L., 2
Bardovi-Harlig, K., 1, 8, 12, 21
Beebe, L., 7, 9, 12
Billmyer, K., 7, 12
Blum-Kulka, S., 7, 9, 12, 21
Blundell, J., 2, 17, 23, 35, 38, 45
Bouton, L.F., 8
Brown, D., 12
Brown, H.D., 82
Brumfit, C., 2, 14-16

Campbell, R., 2
Canale, M., 2
Carrell, P.L., 61, 63
Cohen, A., 12
Cook, V., 2, 6, 20
Corder, S.P., 5, 81

Dahl, M., 7, 45, 63
Davis, K.A., 81
DuFon, P., 7, 12

Ellis, R., 8, 12

Finocchiaro, M., 2, 14-16
Frota, S.N., 7
Fukazawa, S., 12, 21, 78
Ginn, S.B., 38, 40
Guntermann, G., 2

Halliday, M.A.K., 2
Hartford, B.S., 8, 12
Higgens, J., 17, 23, 35, 38, 45
Holmes, J., 12
House, J., 21
Hymes, D., 2

Kasper, G., 7-12, 21, 45, 63

Kerekes, J., 8, 12
Konneker, B.H., 61, 63

Lazaraton, A., 81
Lynch, B., 82

Maeshiba, N., 10, 12
Matsumura, S., 12, 16
McCarthy, M., 3
Middlemiss, N., 17, 23, 35, 38, 45
Murphy, B., 12

Neu, J., 12
Niezgoda, K., 2

Olshtain, E., 7, 9, 12
Omar, A.S., 7, 9
Ozasa, T., 63, 82, 115, 123

Palmer, A., 2
Papalia, A., 2

Richards, J.C., 5, 6, 15, 19-21, 36, 45, 62, 63
Rintell, E., 45
Robinson, M.A., 8, 12
Rose, K., 9, 12
Ross, S., 10, 12
Röver, C., 2

Sasaki, T., 21
Sawyer, M., 8
Scarcella, R., 7, 10, 12
Schmidt, R., 5-8, 11, 15, 19-21, 36, 45, 62, 63
Scollon, R., 16
Scollon, S.W., 16
Siegal, M., 8

133

Svanes, B., 8
Swain, M., 2

Takahashi, S., 7, 11, 12
Takahashi, T., 7, 9, 12
Trosborg, A., 7, 8, 10, 12, 62

van Ek, J.A., 2, 36, 45

Wales, R., 2

Yoshinaga, N., 10, 12

Subject index

A

absolute values, 33
acceptability, 15
acknowledging something for the present, 26, 35, 99
acquisition, 1, 7, 8, 61, 64, 85, 86, 123
acquisitional patterns, 8
acquisitional study, 9
acquisitional research, 8
acquisition studies, 8
adjuncts, 10
adjusted R^2, 43
agreeing, 14, 26, 34, 95, 97-99
analogy, 19
analysis of variance (ANOVA), 6
ANOVA, 51, 68
ANOVA 4, 50
apologies, 5, 10, 12, 62
apologizing, 2, 14
appropriateness, 1, 3, 7, 14-16, 18, 22, 23, 37, 40, 44-49, 53, 54, 56-58, 60, 65, 79, 84, 87, 88, 116, 123
   concept of, 5
   judgment of, 22, 64, 81, 88
   recognition of (the), 18, 37, 44, 46, 60, 64, 84, 85
   referential, 5
   social, 5
   social and stylistic, 4, 18, 83
   stylistic, 5
   textual, 3, 5, 18, 22, 24, 37, 83
appropriateness judgment test(s), 16, 18, 39, 48, 65, 87
approximative system, 19
arguing, 2
arguing back, 35
asking about likes, 26, 34, 39, 98
asking back, 26, 35, 98, 99
asking for information, 27, 95, 96, 98, 99
asking for reasons, 3, 18, 24, 26, 35, 95, 99
asking for someone's opinion, 39, 40
asking if someone is sure about something, 23, 97
asking or giving one's opinion, 27, 34, 83
assertion(s), 78, 80
Assertion Function-chain(s), 39, 40, 44, 55, 56, 60, 67, 69, 84
assertiveness, 12
Assistance Function-chain(s), 39, 48, 52, 53, 60, 66, 68
assistant language teacher (ALT), 40
attracting someone's attention, 96
authentic English material, 38

B

being sarcastic about something, 24, 33, 35, 95, 96
Between Groups, 68-70
between-subjects, 41, 43, 50, 65
blaming someone, 27, 35, 97

C

calling someone's name, 35, 97
calming or reassuring someone, 26, 27, 34, 39, 95, 97, 99
category score(s), 30-35, 87
code component, 2
coefficient of correlation, 28
communication, 3, 13, 15, 19, 21, 35, 83
   internal, 6
communication pattern, 23
communicative approach, 5

135

communicative behavior, 15
communicative competence, 2
　definitions of, 2
　models of, 2
communicative functions, 2
communicative language teaching, 2
communicative purpose(s), 2, 14-16
comparing, 26, 98
complaints, 5, 10, 12, 62
compliment(s), 5, 12, 20
complimenting, 95
conceptualization stage, 16
context(s), 2, 9, 10, 15,
　request, 63
contribution(s), 25, 32
conversation, 6, 14, 24
conversational patterns, 24
corpus, 22, 30, 35
corrected model, 43
corrected total, 43
correlation coefficient, 28
course design
　communicative, 2
Course of Study, 1
covering up a fact, 26, 36, 99
Cronbach's alpha, 38
cross-sectional and longitudinal studies, 8
cross-sectional design, 7, 9, 20
cross-sectional levels, 20
cross-sectional study (studies), 8, 9, 20
cumulative contribution, 25, 32
curriculum, 2

D

data, 4, 18, 25, 41, 45, 49, 65, 81, 115
　appropriate, 35, 87
　a set of, 45
　linguistic, 21
　qualitative, 81
demeaning oneself, 34, 35, 95

denying something, 36, 96
dependent variable(s), 6, 41, 43, 50, 65
descriptive statistics, 41, 42, 45, 50, 65, 66
despising something (someone), 33, 36, 100
design, 11, 42
development, 7, 9, 11, 17, 20, 123
　interlanguage, 11
　interlanguage pragmatic, 7, 13
　pragmatic, 4, 9, 11, 12, 18, 37, 46, 84
　rate and route of, 13, 60, 64, 84, 85
　route of, 18, 44
developmental curve, 13
developmental patterns, 11, 17, 44
df (degrees of freedom), 43, 51-57, 59, 68-70
dialects, 14
dialogue(s), 45, 64, 78, 79
dimension(s), 28-35, 81, 83, 86, 87
disagreeing, 34
disarmer, 21
discourse completion questionnaire, 11
dispersions, 45
downgraders, 10
downtoners, 10

E

educational background, 15
effect(s), 9, 11, 42, 45, 46, 48, 83, 84
EFL(English as a Foreign Language), 6
EFL learners, 1, 7, 61, 64, 77, 79, 80, 85, 88, 123
eigenvalue(s), 27-29, 32, 87
elicitation, 21
emotive force, 45
equal relationship, 39, 47, 117
equals, 10, 78, 79
error, 43, 51, 52
error analysis, 81

Subject index 137

errors
  categories for, 82
  classified table for, 81
  systematicity of, 82
Error df, 42
exact statistic, 42
exchange, 6
exercises, 78
exponent(s), 14-16
expressing confident assertion, 40
expressing dislikes, 26, 98
expressing displeasure
  (at a situation or an utterance), 28, 34, 83
expressing hopes, fears, and so on, 14
Expressing Interest Function-chain(s), 39, 57-58, 60, 68, 70
expressing likes, 26, 39, 98
expressing liking, 78
Expressing Liking Function-chain(s), 39, 44, 53, 54, 60, 66, 69, 84
expressing reluctance to offer assistance, 79
expressing surprise, 27, 95
expressing surprise or excitement, 28, 34, 83

F

F (F values), 42-44, 51, 52, 58, 68-70
factor(s), 2, 14, 16, 22, 25, 26-28, 34, 35, 48, 83, 86
  social, 20
  sociolinguistic, 16
factor analysis, 3, 18, 25, 34, 83, 86
factor loading(s), 25-27, 34, 86
factor rotation, 25
finding out about meaning, 96
first language, 20, 21
formality
  levels of, 15, 17
function(s), 1, 2, 5, 12, 13, 16, 17, 20, 23, 24, 35, 45
functional unit, 19
function-chain(s), 3, 5, 7, 12, 13, 17-19, 22-35, 37-40, 44, 46-52, 58-61, 64, 72-74, 76, 77, 79-81, 83-88, 123
function-chain pattern(s), 23, 38
function-chain structures, 3, 18, 22
function-chain test, 25

G

gestures, 15, 16
getting a precommitment, 21
giving reasons, 26, 97, 99
giving reassurance, 40
giving your opinion, 26, 33, 98
giving yourself time to think, 27, 97
greeting, 24
greeting someone, 33, 94, 96
grounder, 21

H

Hayashi's quantification model III, 3, 18, 28, 29, 31, 32, 34, 83, 86
head act, 21
hedges, 10
hierarchical system, 16
Hotelling's trace, 42
Hypothesis df, 42

I

identifying, 27, 36, 95, 98
illocutionary force, 19, 20
illocutionary meaning, 19
imperatives, 10
implicature, 8
imposition minimizer, 21
independent variable(s), 41, 50, 51, 65
informed consent, 115
input
  pragmatically appropriate, 1
  realistic, 1

Institutional Review Board (IRB), 62, 115
intensifiers, 10
interaction(s), 24, 51, 52, 58
intercept, 42, 43
interjection, 80
interlanguage, 8, 9, 11, 17, 19, 21, 44
interlanguage pragmatics, 7-9, 12, 13
interlanguage system, 19
interviews
  personal, 88
inventiveness in communication, 35, 83
invitation(s), 5, 12
inviting someone, 26, 33, 94, 96, 99

J

justifying oneself, 26, 36, 100

K

kinesics, 15, 16

L

L1, 10, 21, 45
L2, 7, 8, 17, 20, 81
language(s), 1, 2, 5, 7, 9, 13-17, 19, 20, 21, 36, 61, 85, 88, 116
language
  appropriate, 13, 60, 64, 77, 85
  second- and foreign-, 19
  second or foreign, 19
language functions, 5, 12, 13, 20, 85
language use, 1, 2
levels, 41, 50, 65
lexis, 2
linguistic competence, 15
linguistics, 5, 20, 21
linguistic structure, 41, 49
loadings, 27, 28
location, 29, 31, 32
locutionary meaning, 19
longitudinal and cross-sectional studies, 7, 20
longitudinal method, 20
longitudinal study (studies), 7-9, 20

M

main effect, 51
making an excuse (including explaining the details), 26, 27, 35, 96, 97, 100
making a suggestion, 15
making requests, 10
materials, 3
  teaching, 1, 86
matrix (matrices), 4, 25, 65, 81
maximum, 38, 41, 49
mean(s), 6, 30, 38, 41, 42, 49, 50, 52, 54-58, 62, 63, 66-68, 72
median, 38, 45
metalinguistic knowledge, 24, 36
modality markers, 10
morphology, 2
mother tongue, 19, 21
moves
  conversational, 3, 6
  discourse, 3, 6, 17
  follow-up, 6
  opening, 6
  supportive, 10, 12, 21
MS (mean square), 43, 51, 52, 68-70
MSe (mean square error), 53-60
multilingual communities, 21
multiple comparisons, 52-59, 71, 72
multivariate analysis, 35, 87
multivariate analysis of variance (MANOVA), 4, 5
multivariate tests, 42

N

N (sample size), 29, 30, 41, 42, 50, 53-57, 59, 66-68
native language, 21
nominal level, 53-57, 59

O

offers, 5, 12
offering, 14
offering advice, 12
offering assistance, 78
offering to do something for someone, 39
one-way layout ANOVA, 4, 19, 65
one-way layout MANOVA, 18, 41
one-way layout multivariate analysis of variance (MANOVA), 4
order, 5
ordering, 82
output stage, 16

P

p (p values), 42, 44, 51-60, 68-70
paralinguistic features, 15
participant(s), 9, 16, 22, 24, 25, 28, 38, 40, 45, 47-49, 52-57, 61, 63-65, 72, 87, 88, 115, 123
participants
  range of, 4, 18, 44, 46, 64, 84
  study, 88
  test, 46
pattern(s), 4, 12, 19, 22-24, 35, 37, 38, 61, 64, 65, 77, 82, 83
  general, 82
  specific difference, 82
  specific similarity, 82
performance
  interlanguage pragmatic, 9
  pragmatic, 9, 12
  request, 12
performance research, 9
personalities, 15
phonology, 2
Pillai's trace, 42
pitch, 62
politeness 63
  level of, 63
  perception of, 63
politeness levels, 63
politeness values, 61, 63
populations
  learner, 11
post hoc analysis, 52, 58, 72
pragmalinguistic and sociopragmatic knowledge, 8, 20
pragmalinguistics, 20
pragmatic ability, 9
pragmatic assessment, 87
pragmatic competence, 1, 4, 7, 9-12, 19, 37, 40, 44, 49, 61, 87, 88, 123
pragmatic ends, 20
pragmatics, 5, 7, 20, 86
pragmatics studies, 9
preparator, 21
presuppositions, 15, 16
principal component method, 25
proficiency, 4, 10, 11, 18, 37, 45, 46, 84
  L2, 10, 13
  English, 37, 44, 79, 84, 85
  high, 18, 37, 38, 41, 44, 84
  level(s) of, 9, 9-10, 18, 37, 38, 41-44, 46, 47, 50-58, 64, 65, 71, 72, 83, 84
  levels of English, 46, 60, 84
  low (er / est), 11, 18, 37, 38, 41, 44, 84
  low- and high-, 11
proficiency level(s), 9-11, 37, 51, 52, 58, 62, 64
  English, 3-4, 44, 61, 64, 72, 77, 79, 84-86
proficiency test(s), 10, 38
  English, 62
program design, 85
promise of reward, 21
propositional meaning, 19, 20
prosodic features, 48, 62

pseudolongitudinal studies, 11

Q

qualitative analysis, 4, 19, 57, 61, 65, 85
qualitative research, 61, 81
　generalizability of, 81
　role of quantification in, 81
qualitative studies, 81
quantitative analysis, 61, 65
question, 38
questionnaire(s), 10, 48, 115, 116

R

r (number of steps), 53-57, 59
R^2 (coefficient of determination), 43
raw score, 63
Reassurance Function-chain(s), 39, 56, 57, 60, 67, 70
refusals, 12, 20
refusing, 14
rejections, 12
relationship(s), 16, 117
reliability, 28, 34, 38, 86, 87
reporting, 27, 36, 39, 45, 95, 96-98
request(s), 5, 8, 10, 12, 20, 21, 62, 116, 119
request conventions, 11
requesting, 20, 39
research design, 3, 17
respondents, 16
response(s), 23-25, 34, 38-40, 45, 47-49, 72, 77, 80, 115, 116, 123
　appropriate, 41, 49
　compliment, 12
　conversational, 115
　reassuring, 81
　typical, 77, 78, 116
response patterns, 24
role play(s), 10, 11
role relationships, 117
Roy's largest root, 42

Ryan's method, 52, 58

S

sample, 23, 45
satire and scorn, 33, 35, 83
saying how you feel after something has happened, 36, 99
saying someone must not do something, 27, 97
saying something is correct, 26, 27, 96, 98
saying sorry, 27, 96, 97
saying what you prefer, 26, 98
saying what you think is possible or probable, 98
saying you approve, 27, 95, 98
saying you are bored, 24, 33, 95
saying you are curious, 27, 94, 96, 98
saying you are disappointed, 96
saying you are displeased or angry, 27, 39, 96
saying you are excited, 27, 96
saying you are interested, 39, 95
saying you are pessimistic, 24, 33, 94
saying you are pleased, 95, 99
saying you are sure, 23, 39, 40
saying you are worried or afraid, 24, 27, 33, 94, 96
saying you do not approve, 95
saying you do not know, 3, 18, 26, 98, 99
saying you have reached agreement, 95
saying you intend to do something, 26, 100
saying you know about something, 97
saying you partly agree, 26, 98, 99
saying you remember, 26, 98
saying you understand, 35, 96, 97
scale, 30, 31, 45, 48, 85, 116
　ordinal, 45
　rank, 45

scenarios, 16
scoring, 41, 49, 64
scripted speech, 22, 23, 25, 29, 30, 35, 83
second language, 20
second language acquisition (SLA), 7-9, 19, 81
second language research, 21
sequence(s), 3, 17, 24, 62
setting(s), 18, 39, 40, 47-49, 88, 116-122
　classroom, 6
　EFL, 1
　social, 1, 39
shared sociocultural allusions, 15, 16
showing you are listening, 27, 96, 97, 99
significance level, 52-57, 59, 72
significant difference(s), 37, 38, 41-42, 44, 46, 52-60, 72, 84
simple main effect, 51, 52, 58
simple univariate F tests, 43
single-moment studies, 9, 20
situation(s), 1, 2, 5, 6, 13, 15, 16, 19, 80, 115, 116
　communicative, 2, 17
　language use, 1
social relationship(s), 5, 18, 20, 39, 40, 47-49, 72, 77, 80
social roles, 14, 16
sociolinguistics, 5
sociopragmatics, 20
speech act(s), 5, 7, 8, 12, 14, 19, 20, 88
　initiating, 12
　responding, 12
SPSS, 41, 65
SS (sum of squares), 51, 52, 68-70
standard deviation(s) (SD), 30, 31, 35, 38, 41, 42, 49, 50, 62, 63, 66-68
standard score, 62
statement(s), 38, 47
　appropriate, 73, 75

debriefing, 115, 123
statistics, 62
status, 10, 14, 16, 78, 117
　equal, 73-76
　high, 39, 47, 78, 79, 117
　low, 39, 47, 78, 79, 117
status relationships, 16
stimulus (stimuli), 23, 24, 33, 34
strategies, 10, 63
　apology, 10
　apology and complaint, 11
　face, 16
　request, 10, 63
style, 15
　casual, colloquial or familiar, 15
　consultative, 15
　formal, 15
　frozen, 15
　informal, 15
style shift, 15, 16
suggesting, 26, 34, 98
suggestion(s), 5, 12
supportiveness, 12
syllables, 62
syllabus, 5
syllabus design, 20
syntax, 2

T

t (t values), 38, 53-57, 59
talking about what might happen, 26, 27, 95, 96, 100
target language, 11, 19, 20
tasks
　elicitation, 11
telling someone to do something, 96
tense, 20
test(s), 3, 17, 18, 22-24, 29, 31-33, 35, 37-41, 47-49, 60-62, 64, 65, 71, 72, 77, 83, 84, 87, 116, 122, 123
testing, 2, 6

Test of Practical English, 38, 42, 45
tests of between-subjects effects, 43
textbook(s)
  authorized junior high school English, 22
  English, 1, 22, 25, 29, 30, 35, 38, 78, 83
thanks, 12
The Japanese Ministry of Education, Culture, Sports, Science, and Technology, 45
The Society for Testing English Proficiency, Inc., 45
threats, 21
TOEFL, 47
translation(s), 24, 41, 49
trying to change someone's opinion (including arguing back), 24, 26, 33, 95, 98, 100
Tukey's honestly significant difference test, 72
turning something into a joke, 26, 33, 35, 99
two-way layout analysis of variance (ANOVA), 4
two-way layout ANOVA, 19, 49
Type III sum of squares, 43

U

univariate ANOVA, 6

upgraders, 10
usage, 62, 80
use, 3, 5, 7, 12, 20, 80, 115, 116
  L2, 8
use component, 2
utterance(s), 3, 5, 17-20, 23, 24, 37, 46, 79, 87, 116
  appropriate, 87

V

variables, 13, 32, 45
variance, 25, 29, 87
variation, 35, 83
varimax method, 25
validity, 35, 115
value(s), 25, 30, 33, 42, 45
vocabulary, 41, 49

W

warning, 20
warning someone, 98
weight, 30
Wilks' lambda, 42
within-subject, 50
Within Groups, 68-70

Z

z-score(s), 49, 50, 52, 54-58, 62, 65